Altars of REMEMBRANCE

GOD AND THE SINGLE MOM

*with love
and prayer
Hannah*

HANNAH HOFER

ISBN 978-1-64416-588-1 (paperback)
ISBN 978-1-64416-589-8 (digital)

Christian Faith Publishing, Inc.
832 Park Avenue
Meadville, PA 16335
www.christianfaithpublishing.com

Printed in the United States of America

My name is Hannah, and this is a first-person account of a single mother and the hurts and frustrations of raising four children alone and then, three years later, the peace of doing it with the Lord in control of our lives.

The story about the *Altars of Remembrance* is in Joshua 4:7, where God had once again done a miracle and told them to take large stones and build an altar to remember the miracle. Their children would ask what the altar was for, and they could tell them of God's faithfulness. When I asked the Lord what I should name my book, it came very strongly into my mind, *Altars of Remembrance.*

The Lord made it clear to me to write all this and encouraged me along the way not to give up but keep going. The only reason I can think of is for me to share all He did at the lowest points in my life, and then after I put my faith in Him, worked it all for our good. These stories are not just telling of His great love and guidance for His children, but of His awesome protection over them

My more than forty years on staff with Campus Crusade for Christ, now called CRU, has been a blessed adventure, going places and meeting people I would never have imagined. It made me trust my Lord in the most unusual circumstances, each time making my faith grow to new heights. I would not change one moment of it even if I could.

Coming to America

Being in beautiful Switzerland for one year as an exchange student was a joy for this seventeen-year-old. Keeping busy that year in Zurich and learning the Italian language plus recipes from the same friend made the time go by fast. However, being homesick, I was ready to return and was packing to go back home.

My hometown, Augsburg, is a beautiful romantic city in Bavaria, Germany, which still has much of the original city wall intact. A part of the city wall was used as an outdoor theater, with the mote being used to float in small ships for the performances. Augsburg was declared a city in 35 BC by Caesar Augustus, a Roman ruler who was still in power when Jesus was born.

Enjoying Zurich and spending that year with a doctor's family, I got to go with them on vacation in the high Swiss mountains. When my year in Switzerland was up, being homesick made it easy to pack and head back to my family and hug my mom and sisters again.

When I arrived, my mom, my best friend, and her fiancé picked me up, and my friend said she had some good news. Finally, being alone, she told me that she was engaged to Jim, who was a GI soldier. She told me his best friend is a really nice guy and asked if she could bring him the next evening.

Declining, I explained just having broken up with professional Greek football player, and my desire is to first find a good job. Well, she brought him anyway, and after our third outing together, Bill and I had fallen in love. We got engaged three months later and married after the Army okayed it.

The reason this took six whole months was because the Army took all that time to check my background, making sure that no members of my family were involved with the past evil government. My dad, his brother, and six other of my uncles did not come back from that war.

Not until my mom reminded me did I think that marrying Bill meant leaving my family, home, and country. Refusing to see him for two weeks made me realize that I really did not want to spend my life without him, so I agreed to marry him.

Coming to America

A year later, when Bill's time in the Army was up and he needed to return to the USA, we found out that I was three months pregnant. The Army was not going to send me on an eight-day trip across the ocean in a big ship at this early stage.

Since my husband was afraid I would not come over without him, he extended another year. So our little daughter, Lita (Carmelita), was six months old when we left at Bremerhaven to come to the United States.

We arrived in the USA on the USS *Darby* at New York Harbor on January 4, 1959. It was necessary for us to stay five days while Bill was being discharged from the Eleventh Airborne Division. We flew into LAX airport where his family came to pick us up.

Even though I was very homesick, getting comfortable in the US was not hard for me. I liked President Ike and loved the mountains all around San Bernadino, Bill's hometown. Going to the beach was a joy to me, and I learned all about the soccer game they call football.

My English was still not good yet, and when my mother-in-law started talking at the dinner table, I did not know if it was about me. So I went to the library, got myself a language book and tape, and I spoke English in no time.

This started fourteen years of a very happy marriage and three more children, Christina, Stephen, and William, called Billy. My husband and I only had small arguments now and then, and I think it was because we loved making up in the evening. Bill felt very strongly that people should never go to bed angry with each other in case one of them does not wake up in the morning.

Sadly, in the fifteenth year, something began to change. Bill was hardly home anymore, and he was not the same kind and affectionate man he had always been. Knowing something was wrong worried me, but Bill just said it was all the overtime he had to work every night.

A divided family

Our favorite fragrance of gingerbread was once again filling our home and brought wonderful emotions and memories of Christmases past. Lita and Chris, my two daughters, were taking out the batch of cookies from the oven to replace it with the next sheet. The boys, Stephen and Billy, got to play with some of the wooden Christmas ornaments; I did not trust them with any glass ones yet.

With a sudden deep pain, I realized that for the first time in fifteen years, my husband would not celebrate Christmas with us, but in the arms of his twenty-one-year-old girlfriend. Walking to the closet for more ornaments kept my kids from seeing my tears.

Earlier that year, my husband Bill had walked up to me and told me that he wanted a divorce and would come the next day for his clothes. It felt as if all the blood had run out of my body, and so I was unable to move. Little Stephen, two and a half years now, had been playing ball in the kitchen with me, while six-month-old Billy was watching from his baby carrier.

After this announcement, Bill left the house, and little Stephen noticed that the door was not fully closed. The little boy went out and ran down the street after his dad, wanting a ride with him. When Bill came back in the house, I was still frozen on the same spot, leaning against the sink. Pushing his little son into the kitchen, Bill said, "Can you not watch him?" closing the door securely now.

Not remembering the length of time I stood there or what came next, it just seemed like life had stopped. It took me three days to have the strength to tell my girls why their father had not been home and, in my own hurt, didn't recall their reaction.

One of their responses was quitting school and running away from home, so evenings I would pack my two little boys into my small station wagon and drive to the homes of my daughter's friends, those known to me.

However, they never stayed at the houses of the friends I knew, and hearing from some of the mothers that they were on drugs like their own daughters, hurt me deeply. Some of the single moms didn't care about their children having their friends sleeping at their home or out in the garage because they were off with their boyfriends.

The next three years were the most painful of my life; the hardest being sometimes seeing my husband and his girlfriend around town and when they came on Christmas or Easter to pick the children up for an afternoon in their place.

It scared me terribly to raise our four children alone, so I went out dancing with some divorced ladies I had befriended. My hope was to meet some nice man to help me raise my kids.

Discovering soon that none of these men were about to take on a new wife, especially one with four children, it caused me to lose hope; and once the men saw that I wouldn't sleep with them, they lost interest really fast.

One time, being left by one of these gentlemen on the other side of the valley, it took me seven hours to walk home, mostly at nighttime. My sister and her husband had been watching the kids for me and were not very kind at my 5:00 a.m. arrival home.

Having a chance to confront my girls about their choices regarding school and not staying home did not turn out well. When they said that they hoped their dad would look for them and come back home, my heart ached.

It hurt me because there was nothing I could do, so depression set in. Drinking before bedtime made everything worse the next morning because it added the hang-over. However, it was better than the tranquilizers my doc-tor had prescribed for me; they took away all feelings and emotions.

Billy's surgery

When my youngest boy was three years old, he kept running into things right in front of him, and he often held his head saying, "Hurt, Mommy." His head also seemed to be getting larger, so I took him to our doctor, who exam-ined him and told me that he could not see a problem.

However, my little one kept on bumping into things, so taking him to a different doctor seemed the best idea. This one ordered some x-rays and surgery immediately. He explained to me that Billy had what they call hydroceph-alus, or water on the brain. This happened when his tube, which drains the fluid from the brain into the heart, col-lapsed. Therefore, the fluid kept on collecting in the brain.

It made my heart ache to see my little boy on all those big x-ray tables, but he took it without whining or com-plaining. After the long surgery, he was lying in his small hospital bed, but he could not be picked up because his head was heavily bandaged. He also had a small incision on his neck, which was used to feed the shunt from his head into his heart.

When I saw him, my crying was so spontaneous I could not hide it in time; and that sweet child touched my cheek and said, "It's okay, Mommy. It's okay." They made

Billy stay for a week, and thank goodness my job let me work half days; and each day, my girls and I would take turns, staying till he fell asleep at night.

The heartaches continue

Fearing to lose what love there was left between my girls and me, I promised myself not to question them anymore when they came home. However, as I saw in their eyes and hearing in their speech that they had taken dope, my good intentions went out the window.

It was so important to me that they would realize that this is not something they could just walk away from anytime they wanted to. They needed to understand that this will change their lives because it will turn into a permanent habit. I wanted them to know that it will affect the life choices they will make, as well as their physical deterioration.

After another argument, Lita stormed out of the house, yelling that she would not be back again. Going into my bedroom, I dug out my bottle of Darvon, left over from my last hip replacement. Reasoning that someone else would raise my children better than me, I poured most of them in my hand, planning to swallow them.

Suddenly Stephen woke up screaming with one of his bronchitis attacks, and after receiving his medication, he would only calm down by lying in my arms till he fell asleep. After a while, we had both fallen asleep, and my hope was that Lita would come home, and we could make up.

The scenes with my girls did not get any better, but knowing they were acting out in their hurt and confusion made me a little more patient. It was my desire to reach out to them and let them know that I hurt with them and was longing to help.

However, when they came home after they were gone a few days, my anger won. Remembering the agony of trying to find them at night with the two boys in the back of my car, the yelling started again.

Even reading my romance novels every day did not improve my moods anymore. The realities were becoming stronger than the fantasies were. Being together was a constant irritation between us, and neither of us had the courage to say the first kind word. It scared me to think where this would end up if we didn't get some help somewhere.

My job training was finished now, and I found a job at an insurance company because there was no medical job available. The situation at work was really bad; the jealousy and competition was unbelievable, and five o' clock never came soon enough.

It was at that time that Stephen had to undergo a whole series of tests, and again, I ached seeing him poked with so many needles, but it was better than him not being able to breath.

Once a month, he had to take a shot with a really big needle to give him hemoglobin, which, little by little, improved his condition. It was so hard to see his pain and have his little hand reach out to me, wanting my help. At times like these, my longing for someone to confide in and share my problems with grew.

Finally, a special friend

At a friend's Christmas party, I met a man who was very kind and wanted to know me better. After meeting my children, he seemed to be interested in them as well as in me. For the first time in years, someone actually thought I was pretty and a great person to be with. Ben could not have known my need to hear that I was worth knowing.

He made me feel special, and cooking for him his favorite food, especially my European cheesecake, gave me joy. His complements sounded very sincere, and he would always compare me with the roses he brought three or four times a week. It was just like a healing ointment to my low self-esteem, and the kids enjoyed his visits as well. He accepted me just as I was, which made me relax, no pretense or trying to impress him.

My girls said they had not seen me so relaxed since dad left, and we hardly fought anymore. Ben picked me up from work many times and took me to a nice place for dinner and often picked up the kids as well. A real feeling of friendship developed, and I told him that he restored some confidence in myself, making me able to share my hurts and my joys more easily. The notice of Ben having fallen in love with me came too late.

It was selfish to take the things he was doing for me and giving me without returning his love. One day after dinner, he asked me to step outside, and my stomach cramped, having a feeling about what he was going to say. He told me that he wants to get married and had applied for a better job so he could provide for the kids and me and that he was accepted.

It was so hard to tell him that my feelings for him were only friendship and that marriage for me could only come through love on both sides. Assuring him that he was such a wonderful and generous person, he would find the right mate; it would be unfair to him if I pretended to love him just because he was needed.

A new hope

Loosing Ben left an emptiness in my life, and it would have been easy to fall right back into the old depression. However, on the same day Ben left, there arrived a letter from the city's rehabilitation center. They were offering me full-time college training plus payments for childcare, and that gave me some hope.

They said I was eligible because of the hip surgeries and replacements needed for me to walk without a limp again. My choice was medical assistant because that was my job before I got married. They chose a well-known business college for my classes and San Bernardines Hospital for on-the-job training.

My routine was very busy, and I told the kids that this would be only for a year, then there would finally be a good job. This would mean we have some money to go places we always wanted to see. My girls did not trust my promises; I had made many and broke almost all. Why should this be different?

The church I grew up in taught me to see God only as a very strong ruler whom you obey, or there would be no mercy, only eternal torment. In order to get into heaven, my good list has to be longer than my bad list. However, knowing that my good list was not longer than my bad one made me give up on Him.

Because I had not gone to church in a long time, or prayed anymore, my thoughts were that God was punishing me. I had always been told from childhood on that I have to be perfect for God to care. Thinking this is why He let my husband leave me for a much younger woman made it impossible for me to go to Him for help.

Finally, salvation

One day, my mother-in-law had taken my boys to buy them shoes and to spend the night. In my agony, I did not want to face another day of pain and was imagining how to end it all. Lying on my living room floor, screaming out all the hurt of those past three years seemed a long time.

Finally, yelling at God, if He really existed, to help me, a strange peace came over me. Never thinking that He would hear me or even care, sleep finally came.

At about 3:00 a.m. I woke from the front door being closed and realized it was my daughter Lita, who had been gone from home for two weeks. For the first time since her dad left, we sat on the floor and cried and talked about what had happened.

We couldn't understand it since fourteen out of the fifteen years of marriage were so happy. Bill and I hardly ever argued, but if we did, we made sure to make up before bedtime. Bill strongly believed that partners should never go to sleep angry with each other in case one of them would not wake up the next morning.

Since Lita and her friends had snug the keys out of my purse, took my car for a ride, and totaled it, I had lost my job. The only thing left was my Avon route, and on a very hot, middle-of-July day, I took off for my first costumer. Being tired and hot, the young lady opening the door introduced herself as Donna and invited me in for some iced tea.

Answering her invitation to come in and sit down, I told her the reason for being on foot. She replied, "Oh, would you like to give this all over to the Lord?" Having no idea what she was talking about, Donna pulled out a small yellow booklet. It was called *The Four Spiritual Laws*, and she asked to share it with me. Since she was so kind to me, there was no reason for me to be rude and turn her down.

Not quite understanding all she read, but in the prayer, I said that I needed Him, thanked Him for dying for my sins, and asked Him to come into my life and be my Savior and Lord. I thanked Jesus for forgiving my sins and giving me eternal life. Ending with "Make me the kind of person You want me to be" made me feel still and peaceful.

Suddenly I began to weep, imagining that God would give me, such a sinner, a chance to receive His only son and that He would want to live in me. Since I had tried everything else, and my friends and family had drawn back from me, it was time to give God a try.

While the tears were flowing down my face and hanging on her every word, she explained what had happened to me and whom I now belonged to forever. It all seemed like a dream, but I asked Him to come into my heart and life. My life was such a mess; God just had to do better than me.

Donna explained that my salvation was by God's undeserved favor called grace (Ephesians 2:8–9), that I was saved, and that He would clean up my life; it could never be by my effort. Being so ready to be at peace, I believed what He was saying to me.

Not having to get my life in order before God would pay attention to me gave me assurance that my future was in His hands. My decision was, at that moment, not to please everyone else anymore and just be myself, but I realized that I had no idea who I even was.

My questions must not have been very intelligent, but Donna was very patient with me. In spending most of my life trying to please others, it was really great that God assured me of being already what He wanted me to be. This was Jesus's plan when He died on the cross for me and took on my sins.

There is no remembrance of the length of time at Donna's or how I got home, and we had forgotten all about the Avon.

The growth begins

When God loving me became hard to believe, Donna gave me my first Bible and showed me from the scriptures that He wanted me in my present state. It explained that the cleanup of my life had to be His doing, not mine. It was amazing to me, but I truly believed Him.

My mornings were now spent feeding my kids, sending them off to school, and sitting on my couch all day, reading God's Word. Weeping over the things He was telling me, I realized more and more how He truly loved me.

Especially in His Word, He showed me in Romans 8:38–39 that nothing and no one could separate me from His love, not even angels or demons. He also promises in John 10:27–31 that no one can snatch me out of His hand or the Father's hand. Reading daily the Bible Donna had given me began to change my life.

The first gift for reading my Bible daily was my mother-in-law. She strongly disliked me, and this was hard because for the first three years, we had to live with her and his dad till Bill finished the training for his job. His mother did not hide her bad feelings for me and displayed them whenever possible.

When my Bible reading began, suddenly she was my friend and even spoke nice about me to the neighbors. This was the first of many miracles that happened to me and the boys—they also had begun to read the word daily and continued even when they left home to join the Service.

Even their grades, which had been unusually low, began to rise up, and the relationships with their teachers greatly improved. The church summer camps caused some wonderful results. Their attitudes toward church greatly changed, and they were no longer ashamed to pray out loud.

Though I accepted His Word regarding the washing away of my sins, Satan was furious at having lost me. This enemy tried to harass me with attacks of guilt because of the still unhappy lives of my daughters. Guilt is one of Satan's greatest weapons to discourage God's children, but if we refuse him, the Bible says he has to flee.

At times, my remorse about my past would make me feel unworthy to even open my Bible. "Big Christian woman, huh?" Satan would gloat, and I could almost hear him laugh. "Don't you think if Jesus really loves you, that anger would be gone by now? Don't you think you would be a more spiritual mother already?"

Oh, how I cried at these times, thinking of having failed my Jesus again, wanting so much to please Him. My Savior teaches in His Word that I already stand clean in my Father's sight because of what He has done at the cross, and that brought some joy into my life.

Oh, the blood of Jesus

My Lord showed me in the Scriptures that Satan has no more power over me since Jesus's blood was covering me now. There was nothing I could add to that perfect sacrifice, and there was absolutely nothing my now powerless enemy could take away from it.

The best teaching, and the last time I fell for Satan's accusations, was one morning at work, when our director of personnel gave his testimony. Don shared having had this same problem with the devil and how our Savior showed him that it is that blood that has washed us white as snow.

He said the Scriptures tell us to bring up that blood of Jesus because it makes Satan stop; he knows it is that blood that defeated him for all time. He tells us in Hebrews 10:14 that by *one* offering, He has perfected for *all* time those who are justified and are now being sanctified.

Taking this seriously gave me peace again, and I brought up that precious blood every time the enemy shows his ugly head. What a joy. This is how we grow and win one victory at a time. Now, I was on my way again, and the Holy Spirit showed me that He was there all along.

Forgiveness

One of the things the Lord kept putting on my mind was to have a closer relationship with Him by forgiving the people who had hurt me. Strangely, a friend at work just came back from a Bill Gothard seminar, saying that it really helped her.

Knowing my past, Donna paid for me to attend this seminar right away and watched my boys for me. Attending it fully convinced me that this was what my Savior was telling me to do. He impressed on me strongly to start with the most important one, my ex-husband, Bill.

Trying to find an easy way out, I realized that there was none because of my desire to be closer to this God who loved me. Starting to dial several times, I finally finished all the way; my hope was he would not answer. Asking Bill to forgive me for whatever part I had in him losing his love for me was hard.

However, he answered, and after asking him, he said flippantly, "Yeah, if it makes you feel better, I forgive you," and hung up. As I hung up the phone, anger started to rise in me saying, "Who forgives whom here?" But as soon as the thought had come, I asked the Lord to forgive me.

This is why I love it when my Savior says in Jeremiah 29:11 that He knows the plans He has for me, and that they are plans for good, not for evil, to give me a future and a hope. I kept using this on cards for birthdays, sympathy, or congratulations because Him promising them hope gives me joy.

Just a moment later, a sweet feeling of relief flowed over me for having been obedient. Thanking my God for having chosen this new life for me ages ago in spite of my failures and detours, He already knew the ending of His plan for me.

My girls had noticed that something had changed in my life but still didn't quite trust it to be permanent. It started in July 1974, which began an unbelievable life of walking with my Lord and trusting Him for our needs.

However, He also wanted me to trust Him with the salvation of my four children and the rest of my nineteen family members. This began a time of praying for each of them every day by name, adding friends and new family members as they came into my life.

But my loneliness was still there, and at times, along with reading the Bible, I kept on spending time in my romance novels, and I had boxes full of them. Those were the times I wanted to go out and date again.

One day, God clearly impressed on me that my replacing time with Him and His Word with imaginary love affairs was sad to Him. When He kept bringing up the scripture saying, if your eye offends, you pluck it out, I asked the Holy Spirit to explain it to me, and He made it clearer.

He told me that these novels were a trap and a hindrance to me, and they must be removed from my life. I went out into the garage and packed up all romance novels and took them to a dumpster, deciding never to read one again.

Still temptations

This was not the end of my learning, and I began to see that these trials and teachings were valuable because after each one, there was more strength and a little more wisdom. While learning the great love of my Savior, there was also a getting wiser to the tricks of the enemy.

There was a weekend coming up, and it was advertised that they had planned a series of romantic movies, all with my favorite actor. Setting up snacks separately for the kids and me, they were told not to bother me except in commercials.

The dishes were done early, and it was time to turn the TV on and get involved in stories other people had dreamed up. To my great shock, the TV screen was blank, and no matter what we tried, it would not play.

Calling my sister and asking if I could come and watch the on either of their two TVs, she informed me that one was broken. She said on the other one, they were watching their favorite football team this weekend.

My best friend was away on vacation so there was no chance to watch these movies. So I spent a lovely weekend with my kids, and we saw a great movie at my church put on Saturday night after a potluck dinner. After church on Sunday, we had a nice lunch at our favorite park.

On Monday morning, the kids turned on the TV, and not being surprised, it turned on and played with no problem or adjustment needed. I was laughing out loud because it was unbelievable to me that this God who loved me would go through all this trouble to improve my life.

He also brought to my mind that He did so much more than this by promising that if He goes and prepares a place for us, He will come again and receive us to Himself and that where He is, there we may be also.

So again the message was clear from my beloved God, and my time in His Word became a daily habit. Now, there were less times of loneliness until finally, His Word began to fill my mind, and there were none.

The healing starts

My girls and their boyfriends were the first to follow me into the kingdom by receiving Jesus Christ as their Savior, but the rest of my family wanted nothing to do with me yet. They said to keep my God to myself and yelled at me never to talk to them about Him.

Donna had been taking my kids and me to her church, Community Bible Church, and they welcomed us. In spite of the divorce, they accepted us and made us a part of their fellowship. We attended every function and service the church had, not getting enough of the wonderful messages the pastor gave about this God.

Stephen and Billy joined the youth club called AWANA, and not to be left out, I became a leader for the high school girls. The scriptures we had to memorize in those days are still in our minds today, and all three of us received many trophies.

It was years later, at Stephen's wedding, that their wedding planner told them about a lady named Hannah with their last name. She shared with them that this lady was the reason she and her sister still walked with Jesus and still attended that same church.

She continued to explain that she and her sister attended AWANA but always came late because there was no one who would bring them so they walked all the way from home. Well, someone was found to bring them, and Hannah would take them home after and tell them more about this Jesus they came to know.

Of all the reasons that God had me there, this was one of them, and we never know the wonderful plan of our Savior for our lives until we are willing to be used. We don't have to have major training or years of great experience, just willingness. He uses us and gives us the right words to say.

The Lord's loving work

There were still some bad scenes with my girls, but not as nasty or as long. God began to answer my prayers, and I was grateful. Asking Donna, she explained through scriptures that the healing of our past needs time in order to be permanent.

The truth about the Lord's unconditional love and total forgiveness began to filter more and more into my self-condemned heart. It made me able to forgive my daughters sooner and myself as well. Wanting so much to be His example, I began to practice it, especially on my own daughters.

The recurring problems in their marriages came from the same reason—they were not able to trust each other or God yet. It would make me fall back in the old trap of worrying, but the Holy Spirit began His work in us. I finally admitted this to a few friends at Sunday school, and we began to bring it seriously before the Lord.

My patient God had to convince me each time that He loved them more than I ever could. All He wanted me to do was to love them and pray; the changing would have to come from Him and in His own timing. He helped me by letting my spirit become less judging.

The Lord showed me in His Word that unless He did the work of renewing by the Holy Spirit, the growth would not only be impossible, but it would not be permanent. I promised by faith to do better, pleading with my Savior for help in this.

So I put them, as well as myself, once again back into His so capable hands and realized that His work will be for all eternity. This is why it was slower than I liked. The very best I could do for them was to continue to approach the throne of God on their behalf and make it a daily habit.

Standing on His promises

There were times when I truly had to stand on my Savior's promises, not on feelings. Remembering that Jesus Christ said He came so that we would have an abundant life right here and now, I began to believe that and claimed it as well.

This promise I made invalid by allowing the enemy to throw me into doubt every time His work does not make sense to me. Trusting Him totally still needed more work, of me surrendering everything into His capable hands and truly leaving it there.

Chris was to meet with her manager one afternoon, and we waited at Lita's home in case Chris needed me that night. Little Christopher was with me to take him to her when she was done. When we had not heard from Chris by 8:30 p.m., I inquired at her job and was told that she had left over an hour ago, having been terminated.

Asking the Lord to keep my heart and mind still, and acknowledging that He knew exactly her whereabouts, I quieted down. Surely He had shown me His faithfulness by now, and would I not be able to trust Him? It was time to drive home because Christopher needed to be in bed.

The ringing of the phone startled me, it being 1:30 a.m. Sleepily I answered, expecting it to be Chris. She was crying, telling me this was more than she could handle. God would have to pull her out of this mess. She could not go on like this. Amazed at the calmness of my heart, I assured her that the Lord still loved her, knew all about it, and cared for her deeply.

Sharing about my similar situation when I was just saved and did not know Him personally yet, and when I finally cried out to Him for help, my Lord was there, and He took care of everything. All our loving God wanted was my surrender to His will, but He was not going to push me. It had to be my choice.

While struggling and fretting, He could not take control because my attention was not on Him. It would be a matter of putting aside my pride and asking Him to take over and let Him be in control once again. In the Bible, He tells us that the name of the Lord is a strong tower. The believer runs to it and is saved.

He also promises that he who calls on the name of the Lord shall be saved, and again, he who comes to Him will in no wise be cast out. Feeling like God wants nothing to do with me is always wrong.

Putting my feelings aside, I could claim His glorious promises because He says that He never lies. Chris had stopped crying and sounded calmer after this. She asked me to keep Christopher till the next day.

The next morning, my mom was having breakfast with me, and she expected me to be worried about Chris like she was. However, my view was now from a different perspective—namely, the Lord's, and so I would wait on Him.

Describing to my mom that my peace in the midst of this storm is from knowing that God loves Chris so much he longs to reveal this love to her, but she has to receive it. So working this out had to be in His hand, not in mine.

The only thing for me to do was to place this child of mine back into His outstretched arms and laying my motherly heart open before Him. Oh, how good it is to know that He takes care of all we entrust to Him, especially our children. He tells us to cease striving and know that He is God.

Two days after this, Chris's problems were taken care of. She did not have to leave her apartment, and she got an offer for a better job. Chris was more at peace after this and began to trust this God she was coming to know.

That weekend, we were celebrating my nephew Gary's wedding, and all the family was together. Suddenly they played a popular song called "Daddy, Daddy, Don't You Walk So Fast."

It was a song about a little boy running after his dad when he is leaving his family. This song used to tear up my heart, reminding me of little Stephen running after his dad when he left us.

Lita came and found me, and knowing my hurt, she put her arms around me and held me. With gratefulness to my Lord, I realized that I had not thought about that situation in a long time and knew that the healing of it would continue.

My sister Magdalena

We called my youngest sister, Maggie. She, too, had married an Army man. They had three children and were stationed in Houston, Texas. While her husband was away on tour of duty, she and the girls came to stay with my mom for a month. They were also on my daily prayer list, and I asked my beloved Savior to give me the opportunity to share with them His plan of salvation.

Well, true to our faithful God, the chance came in their first week with us. My mom paid for us to spend three days in a lovely cabin in our San Bernardino Mountains. One day, while Maggie was sleeping in, her three girls and I took a walk.

Strolling through the beautiful forest, we sat on a big log on the side of the path. The Holy Spirit whispered, "An open door, Hannah," and I got the message. It was a joy to me that they listened intently as I explained Jesus's love, which He had for them since long before they were born.

Telling them that He said that before He made the world, He knew them and chose them, I continued with the awesome suffering and the kind of death he endured just so they could live with Him in the most beautiful place forever.

When asked, all three agreed to give Jesus their lives, and so we prayed the salvation prayer, and we hugged because now we were sisters forever. I promised to buy Bibles for them the first chance we got. They were really happy, but not as much as this aunt who got more of her prayers answered.

My chance with Maggie came two days later, and to my surprise, she also listened with the same outcome and without questioning any of what she heard. My sister also received Jesus as her Lord, and she said she had seen the peace in my life and wanted that in hers.

We rejoiced together because they were in a whole new family now, and we celebrated with a special dinner and dessert. They also prayed for their dad's salvation with me, and we thanked God in advance, believing in Him answering our prayer.

It was a very emotional farewell when they left, and we promised to visit sooner this time. The next day, Maggie called me and shared a miracle with me. Before they boarded the plane, she asked the Lord to take away her smoking habit; all her adult life she tried to quit but could not do it. She asked Him, now that she belonged to Him, would He please help her.

As she continued, she began to cry, telling me that from the moment she left the plane, expecting to light a cigarette, she had lost all desire. Even the rest of the day and evening, as well as the next day, there was a bad taste in her mouth when she thought about having a smoke.

When I called her two days later, she said how grateful she was to the Lord who loves her so much He took away a habit she had since she was sixteen. It was a joy to me that she knew who to thank for that.

Learning to tithe

Reading the first time about tithing brought questions to my mind. Never having heard about it, my questions were answered by Donna. She told me that the Lord said in Malachi 3:10, "Bring the whole tithe into the storehouse so there will be food in My house and to test Me now in this if I will not open for you the windows of heaven and pour out for you a blessing until it overflows." That sounded so awesome to me.

However, what impressed me even more was that He promises to rebuke the devourer for our sake so that he cannot destroy what is left. This means that He will not let Satan mess with and destroy what is left over after I give Him the 10 percent that are His.

This happened to me many times, but two of them I will share to give you the idea. It was payday, but it was not a full check, so my plan was not to tithe this time. We went to the store to get some groceries, and while checking out, we talked excitedly about the evening program at our church.

As we drove out of the parking lot, we realized that we had forgotten the bags of food. Turning around and quickly going in the store, we found out someone had already taken he bags. They were not set aside; they were taken. Checking out the receipt, it was to the penny what I should have tithed this payday.

Another time, having read Malachi chapter 3 again, my friend invited me to a missionary couple speaking at her church. Their need really touched me, and my heart went out to them. The only money in my purse was a twenty-dollar bill, and it was to pay my electric bill the next day.

However, my heart longed to give it, so I dropped it into the church's offering basket. Satan calling me a fool did not faze me; I refused to listen to him. The next day, it was Monday and was my day to volunteer at the Campus Crusade for Christ mail system. This was a year before the Lord gave me a job there in the hotel.

One of my precious coworkers came up to me and handed me an envelope. She said, "The Lord gave my husband and me extra this month, and He told us to give it to you." My heart rejoiced when I opened it because it was $19.85 to the penny, the amount of my electric bill. God always supplies in unknown and wonderful ways, and all the glory goes to Him.

The trip to the San Diego Zoo

My children had asked for a while to go to the San Diego Zoo, so on a Saturday after payday, we took the two-hour trip. Lita asked if she could bring one of her friends. I agreed, and so the car was full. It was a beautiful scenic drive, passed an Air force base, farms, hills, and old California mansions.

We brought a nice picnic to eat before entering the zoo so we would not have to buy food while inside. We had so much fun looking at God's awesome creations, admiring some and laughing at others. The time went by much too fast, but I wanted to drive home while there was still a little daylight until I was in familiar territory.

Suddenly I saw that my gas odometer was on empty because the warning light came on. Telling the kids to look for a gas station, I remembered that, due to gas shortage at that time, the gas stations closed at 5 p.m., and it was 6:00 p.m. now. We found two of the most common ones, and sure enough, they had the signs up: *Closed at five.*

Well, we realized it would be foolish to look for more gas stations, and after some prayer, we decided to head for home and trust the Lord. What concerned me was that a really big part of that ride home was past hills and a few farms. We also had to drive past March Air Force Base, so there were no gas stations anywhere.

Trying to be calm and not let the kids worry, these precious young people claimed that they could feel God push our car with His little finger. The needle for the gas had been totally past the empty line since we left San Diego City one and a half hours ago.

Entering Riverside, I got off the freeway, figuring it was safer on the city streets when the car would slow down. Finally, it did slow down near a gas station, and pulling in, the car coasted and stopped at one of the pumps. The kids started jumping out of the car, yelling, "It's open! It's open!"

Sure enough, a man walked up and offered to put gas in my car and explained he was working on his car. He said he totally forgot to close up the station. We told him our dilemma, and he began to laugh so hard we had to join in. He said, "That is just like our God."

He shared having had a similar situation, and being a believer the Lord helped him also. After rejoicing another few minutes, we each thanked our loving God for, once again, taking care of us, and headed home, never forgetting that blessed trip.

Something valuable

One of the first lessons I learned from my favorite teacher was hard to follow. When my daughters were on their own and had money problems, my mom and I jumped in to helped out. This shortage happened more and more, and I could see that they were not wise in the use of their money. So I counseled with my teacher.

As he answered me, I remembered my pastor also having given a message on this called, "Tough love." Both gave the same strong advice, which was that we are not helping but harming them. He said that the Lord loved them and needed to teach them responsibility, but my Mom and I were interfering with His lesson.

God was showing me then that they were not relying on Him, but on us, and so would not learn this valuable teaching. My stopping the help caused them to do exactly what my teachers said they would do—get angry with me.

My mother would not stop running when they asked for help and refused to listen to what I shared with her. Finally, the Lord took her job away, which was not pleasant to Him, but it was to disable her from interfering with His lesson for their lives.

After neither of us helped anymore, both girls found jobs in walking distance, and now it was all right for us to help out a little but only once in a while. Shortly my mom got a nice job again, and she saw that God always has the best plan.

Besides my pastor, my favorite teacher has always been Chuck Windowsill, and I listened to his messages every morning and taped them as well. He always taught only from the Bible, and I could not get enough. I learned from Chuck that my life is 10 percent of what happens to me and 90 percent of how I respond to it. It depends on my response to the things that happen to me, and I shared this with others.

Bill's stroke

My daughters were married now, and their husbands had also received Christ, but they didn't come to church, and soon didn't attend our Bible studies anymore. We were praying for them daily and trusted the Lord to do His precious work in their hearts.

One day, in 1977, my daughter Lita came home and told me that her father was going to marry his current girlfriend and planned to go to court and ask for partial custody of our two boys.

My heart ached for them; they were only eight and ten, and it scared me to think how confusing their lives might be now that they would be divided between Bill and me. We had Bible studies every day, and the TV did not go on until we spent at least half an hour in God's Word, and I saw the Lord bless this.

So when Lita came and told me about it, fear entered my heart; but this time, I knew what to do. Grabbing my Bible, I dropped on the couch, asking God for help because of my still limited knowledge of His Word.

While crying and talking with the Lord, my Bible had fallen open. When I looked down, my eyes fell on God's Word, and it told me in Isaiah 54:4–10 not to fear. He promised that I will not be put to shame, neither be humiliated, nor be disgraced. He said I will forget the shame of my youth, and the approach of my widowhood, I will not remember.

He also revealed in verse 5 that my husband is my Maker, whose name is the Lord of hosts, and my Redeemer is the Holy One of Israel, who is called the God of all the earth. He showed me in verse 6 that He called me, like a wife forsaken and grieved in spirit, even like a wife of one's youth when she is rejected.

My whole body shook with sobs as I began to realize what my newly found Savior God was saying to me. Finally, I was able to continue reading, and my eyes saw how He continued to comfort me.

God promised in verse 13 that my sons will be taught of the Lord, and the well-being of my sons will be great. He said that in righteousness, I will be established, and I will be far from oppression, for I will not fear from terror, for it will not come near me.

Bill doing this would mean I would have to go to court again, and it scared me. However, I listened to what else He said in verse 15 that if anyone fiercely assails me, it will not be from Him. Whoever assails me will fall because of me. He continued that no weapon that is formed against me shall prosper, and every tongue that accuses me in judgment will be condemned.

Not knowing enough of God's Word, I thought He meant this only for Israel until He convinced me otherwise. He closed with this being the heritage of the servants of the Lord, and their vindication is from God.

There was an overwhelming peace that flooded my heart and soul because I was absolutely sure of being His servant. My trust would be in my Lord this time, and closing my Bible, I went to sleep.

Four days later, I received a phone call from my mother-in-law that Bill had a stroke and was in the hospital, totally paralyzed on the left side. Picking up the boys from school, we went to see him, but we were not allowed to go in because he was in a coma.

Not until a week later, we got permission to go in his room and were told that he could hear us, even though he would not respond. So I kept sharing the gospel with him and told him how he could be sure to spend eternity with God.

When Bill had the stroke, he lost his job, and child support was no longer coming to me as a help with the boys. This did not scare me at all. By now, I had enough knowledge about my God to know that all would be well. Even my girls said to my mom, "This will not worry our mom. God always takes care of her."

More protection

One evening, the kids and I were on the way to pick up some tomato plants for the garden, which my boys had started for me. Our stomachs were also telling us that we were past dinnertime so we were going to grab some food as well. Coming up H Street, I stopped at the Stop sign before entering Kendall, planning to turn left and go over Little Mountain.

There was a very long truck coming down the mountain, giving the turn signal and getting ready to turn into the street we were on. When I could be sure he was really turning, I started out to turn left into Kendall and go up the mountain.

Suddenly there came a car flying out behind the truck, and as I hit the brakes, the car swerved over to its left into the dirt, missing us by inches. That car had been totally hidden by the huge truck and was passing in the opposite, illegal lane, and it just kept on going.

Taking a deep breath, we all agreed that only a mighty hand could have moved that car to keep from hitting us full force. Being grateful to our God for saving us would be a great understatement. We still went to pick up some dinner, but our appetite had shrunk, and we wanted no tomato plants that day. We just sat and praised our God for keeping us save once again.

My job at Campus Crusade for Christ

Not receiving child support meant I had to find a job. Before I was married, my work was as a medical assistant, and I had just taken additional college classes at San Bernardino Valley College before Bill's stroke. My job applications were all over San Bernardino and Riverside County, and I was asking the Lord to lead me to the right one.

Coming home from one of my job interviews, very tired, I plumbed down in a chair, asking my beloved God why He had not let me find one. Being sure that He would find me one, I was confused about His timing but was not doubting His willingness.

About an hour later, a phone call came through, and the caller introduced himself as being with Campus Crusade for Christ. He asked me if I was still looking for a job. They had no job application from me there, thinking that God would need me out in the world to tell them the good news.

Answering yes, he asked full-time, to which I again agreed. To my surprise, he told me to come in this following Monday morning and report to the accounting department. Reminding my beloved Savior of being a medical assistant, I wondered what I would do in accounting?

Well, Barney, a very nice gentleman from my new church was my supervisor, and he patiently began to teach me how to do accounts receivable. Going home crying the first few days, I became more and more familiar with it and actually began to like it.

After five years, however, I asked the Lord to please give me some more spiritual work and was transferred to the ministry's fundraising department. Working with our precious donors, I got to inform them of our great success. This was due to using our Jesus film and because of their generous giving.

My department was named financial development, and my job was calling our donors, encouraging them, and praying for them. The field staff gave me the awesome reports of the work God was doing through our staff, which are in every country of the world.

This is a film Campus Crusade for Christ had produced in the Holy Land using only the Gospel of Luke. The film was in 1,200 languages in those days. Our records showed that more than 6.3 billion had seen it, and most had received salvation. A children's version was made later, and my great-grandchildren watch it almost every day.

In doing this work, my own joy and faith were always at a high, especially when the Lord gave me also some personal ministries in the evenings and on weekends. The first one was teaching Sunday school at my church. This I truly loved, and God gave me the desire to work with young people ever since.

The thing that greatly blessed me in those early days was that Campus Crusade highly encouraged reading the Bible every day. This truly fit in with my strong desire to know and trust my God more. We were allowed to read the Word of God the first half hour of our workday.

Arrowhead Springs

My first seventeen years were working at the beautiful Arrowhead Springs Hotel on the foothills of the San Bernardino Mountains. There is no way for me to describe my joy in driving up and down the hill every day, going past those very big and ancient pine trees leading up to the entrance.

This hotel is located directly below an enormous arrowhead that has grown on the face of the mountain.

This arrowhead is behind the hotel and points directly to it, and it is natural, not man-made. The hotel has a very interesting history, especially about the very hot and healing waters under its grounds.

It is well-known especially in Hollywood due to some of the most famous actors having stayed there. Dr. Bill Bright purchased the hotel to use as headquarters for the ministry he had started in Hollywood. My beginning there was in June 1977 when the Lord gave me a job there.

Ever since then, this property has been holy ground for me, having found salvation by one of their employees and spending time there even after work hours. Our house had a swamp cooler, and when it got hot in the summer, all that came out was warm, humid air.

So after work, I would go home, grab peanut butter sandwiches and Kool-Aid, and my boys and went back up to the hotel. We would stay in the pool till the temperature had cooled down, and we could go back home.

Those were awesome years, especially when music teams spent time there and came to the side of the pool to practice for their upcoming tours around the US and the world. It was indescribable to be in the beautiful fifty-meter, Olympic-sized pool. Its water comes from natural hot springs and has to have regular water added to cool it down.

We were able to listen to inspirational music, much of it written by Bill and Gloria Gaither and performed by Christian artists. My favorite is still *Today, the Sky Shall Unfold*. It was not hard to imagine heaven being just like that, with people loving God and each other, living together in perfect peace.

My favorite times where having my lunch every work day under a huge old pine tree on top of the outdoor theater. Then I would read my Bible till the time was up. God became very real to me at this place as His Word kept speaking to me, revealing His wonderful truth.

My oldest son and my youngest daughter each had their wedding at the romantic chapel on the hill and had their receptions in the Roman Room. Five of my family members worked at the hotel and loved it. My oldest son had a job there as a security guard when he finished his Army time. My youngest nephew, Mike, also worked there in security.

One of the exciting times we had at the hotel were the hours we spent at the steam caves. These also got their steam from those hot underground creeks, which would come above ground on many places and be used for health reasons. This beautiful, historic hotel has some wonderful memories for my family members and myself and pictures to go with the stories.

More training

Donna was discipling me, and she knew of my hunger for a greater knowledge of God, and so she arranged and paid for me to take an IBS course. This was an intense study in the Old and New Testament. Dr. Kaiser was an excellent teacher of the Old Testament, and he brought it to life. My classes were much too short; I wanted more.

In the afternoons were the New Testament classes, and it was hard for me to believe how much I had missed all my years growing up. It gave me a deep insight in the nature of the God I had come to love.

Two of my teachers, Mr. and Mrs. Verbeff, became very dear to me. I loved the way they made the Christian life sound possible. Sitting next to his mother one time, I told her that I asked the Lord to let my sons turn out just like hers.

After eight years of rejection by my family, telling me to keep my God to myself and not witness to them, they finally, one by one, began to have questions about this Lord I loved and worshipped and began to attend church with me or someone else.

My nephew, Mike, was the first to ask Jesus to be his Lord and Savior with me, and almost every Sunday, Mike would call me and tell of another one who went forward to receive Christ. Most of them, even four of my grand-children and seven of my great-grandchildren, would get baptized at my church, Immanuel Baptist.

All my children have attended this church and have grown by Pastor Rob's teaching, always according to God's Word. My years as AWANA leader there were a blessing. I had the junior high school students on Sunday night and the high school students on Monday night, and it felt like these kids were a gift from God.

When my mother and sister got baptized there and admitted that they received Jesus as their Savior and Lord, my tears just flowed. This was a dream of mine, and now it came true. Figuring they would be the last to enter the kingdom of God, it brought unbelievable joy to my heart to see them saved.

It all started with my four children, eventually in-law children, my eight grandchildren, and finally, sixteen great-grandchildren, except for the two youngest, which I gave another year. Then I would explain the salvation process even though they already knew about Jesus. What a joy to be used for passing on all the wonderful news of God's love and forgiveness.

The fire at our house

One day, my daughter Lita called, saying that her husband's tire busted and asked if they could borrow my spare. Stephen and our puppy were contently sleeping, so I took Billy and rushed off two streets over to take the tire and the tools. We were almost done when we saw two fire trucks go rushing past the bottom of the street we were in, slowing down and going up some street close by.

We left everything and went to check how close they were and, with total shock, saw that they were not only on our street, but were parked in front of our house. Stephen came running down the street, our puppy following him, and my heart was relieved.

While we stood in front of our house and watched the fire being put out, it was so amazing the total peace that filled my mind and heart. My learning about the awesome faithfulness and provision of our God earlier kept me from falling apart.

However, now in my first big trial since the Lord saved us, I was sure that all would be well. There was nothing left of the garage or anything in it, no ceiling or roof anywhere on the house except over the three back bedrooms.

So we gathered what we could carry of whatever was not damaged by the fire or the water. Calling Donna, she said she would see if we could stay at the Arrowhead Springs Hotel until my insurance would come through with a place to stay. There were actually seven of us right now; my son in law had lost his job, and so they had lost their apartment.

Staying in my four-bedroom house would not have been a problem, but we did not count on the fire. We were very grateful when Campus Crusade allowed us to stay in the dorms and would even provide our meals.

Visiting our house the next day, we noticed that the fire had gone exactly to where the crack in the ceiling had ended, so there were roof and ceiling over all three bedrooms; nothing was damaged in them.

It took me a few minutes to realize that my awesome God had stopped the fire smack-dab where the damage had ended and that our entire home would have a brand new roof and ceiling. After five days at the hotel, the insurance rented us a small apartment one street over from our house for as long as the repairs would take.

However, now in the small, two-bedroom apartment, the seven of us were really crowded, but we did the best we could. Finally, we were out of any kind of meat and out of toilet paper, but this time, we decided not to tell anyone our need but trust the Lord to provide.

That afternoon came a knock on our door, and there was a lady that I knew some time ago but had not seen her for about two years. She put down two big grocery bags on the table and explained why she was here. She had looked for me at my house, and the repairmen told her where we are living for a while.

She began to unpack the grocery bags and explained that her husband only liked his meat from a special store. However, this time another grocery store had a meat sale going on, and so she went there. Her husband was furious, but she was not willing to take all that meat back. She said, for some reason, I came to her mind to share her purchases with.

Here she had unloaded package after package of the best kind of meats, nothing but roasts and steaks and chops. We had not seen any good meat like that in a while, and we were grateful beyond words. The most blessed thing to us was that this lady had no way of knowing our need, but we knew who brought me to her mind.

One hour later, my mom stopped by with a bag full of toilet paper she got at a sale. Our needs were once again taken care of, and we expressed our gratefulness to the God of love. I could never have imagined that my life would be so content and at peace due to my Savior's constant care.

Finding the insurance papers for the house after the fire, the insurance agent said that our policy was only for the structure. This meant no carpets, no curtains, no burned fence, no washer or dryer, no ruined couches, or chairs, or any furniture would be replaced. However, peace did not depart from us; we had seen the goodness of our God.

However, to make an awesome story short, everything was replaced, even the fence and its gate and the whole kitchen counter, which was porcelain tile. Somehow a small crack had occurred, and a tiny piece of tile missing made them replace the counter along with the sink.

When we came home, we just stood and gazed at our new house, praising God and amazed at all that was new. The wallpaper in the kitchen had a little smoke damage; I had never liked that paper but didn't want to go through the terrible job of scraping it off.

The man in charge of the repairs said that they would remove the wallpaper but that they were not allowed to replace it. They would instead paint the wall any color I wanted.

God has never stopped providing for us and often with more than just our needs, so our faith grew to beautiful heights. No new trial could bring us fear because God continued to show us His faithfulness and His love. This made us believe and trust in His promises by reading His Word whenever possible.

The Panorama fire

Having been home from the hospital for three days, I had become more familiar with getting around with my walker. About 7:00 a.m. Billy had gone outside to feed the rabbits and came back in, telling us that there is a big fire in the hills north of us.

Following Billy and Stephen outside, Chris and I went to see the fire. We stood and watched in awe how it spread rapidly across to the north range, but no one was concerned so we went back inside. It was about 10:30 a.m.

when Chris came in from the backyard, describing the way the fire was now beginning to creep over the hills.

It had started to eat its way up the backside of the hills, now coming toward the homes in the foothills in our direction. During this time of year, the Santa Ana winds began to pick up as they did now and became a serious problem. This always means piles of sand on our windowsills, so we closed all the windows.

By noon, the winds had greatly increased, and since Christopher was taking a nap, Chris used my car to quickly get some needed groceries. She was hoping to be back home before the baby woke because I could not pick him up yet.

From this time on, things happened very fast. The winds had increased even more, and because of the sand and smoke being whipped around, it was impossible to see how far the fire had come. My neighbor's son from across the street, knowing that I was still immobile, came to inform me that the fire had reached the foothills, and the schools were being evacuated.

While thanking him with a pinch in my stomach, I realized that there was no way for me to pick Billy up from school, and it would be a long way for him to walk home in this terrible wind. The danger of my situation became real to me as the thought hit that there was no way to get Christopher and me out of the house.

So once again, I called on the Lord for our protection, and His awesome peace returned, knowing that He was fully aware of the whole situation. Just then, Chris pulled into the driveway and, in her usual foresight, had already picked up her youngest brother and rushed home to take us all to safety.

She had seen some of the houses already being consumed on the north end of our area. Chris had gotten back just in time and was hurrying the boys, Christopher, and me into the car to get to my sisters.

Calling Stephen's school was the first thing I wanted to do when we got to our destination to find out where the bus would drop him off. Because of the fire, the bus could not stop near our house as usual but would have to stay below the police barricades.

We had called my sister, Karin, and her husband, Harold, about our arrival, and they had already counted on it. Their home was in Del Rosa and seemed to be far enough away from the fire site. When we got there, a friend had already let Stephen off, figuring that the bus could not take him near our home.

In my mind, I was giving my Savior Jesus a big hug, knowing that this was a gift to me. However, the excitement was not over for the day. Suddenly Chris announced that she could not just simply stand by and let our home of twenty-one years go up in flames.

My screams of protest were of no use since she had already jumped in the car and was pulling out of the driveway. My mother, who lived with my sister, tried to console me, reminding me that there were police barricades everywhere. She did not know my Chris very well; she was too much like me in being aggressive and bold.

She knew every little side street that would get her to our home. Placing her once again in the hands of the God who loved her was easier this time, with knowing that He would be there with her. He assured me He would take care of her, and I became still and let Him be God.

About twenty minutes later, the call came from Chris, and she was crying, telling me that our house would be next because the one just before us was smoldering from some sparks having landed on its roof. My yelling for her to get out of there worked this time, telling her I did not care about the house, only about her.

She replied that the police were making her get out, and some firemen had just entered the yard. Suddenly an overwhelming thought hit my mind. In all the hurry of getting out of the house, we had forgotten all about our three pets. One was a canary called Woodstock and the boys' two rabbits.

Trying to reach Chris would be of no use because she would have left the house by now, and my heart ached over having to tell my boys about their pets. The following morning, the sheriff's department notified us that it was safe to return to our home; and it being Saturday, we were ready in no time.

We had to go home the long way because not all streets were open yet, so we followed instructions. We all held our breath as we approached home, but the house looked clean and whole as when we left. Our greatest delight was hearing our beautiful canary just singing away, as if we had just been to the grocery store.

Billy came running inside, carrying his bunny, saying that Stephens was under the rose bushes eating the grass. Our gratefulness to the Lord was endless. Once again, He proved to be so faithful. How could we ever repay His goodness?

Even when we checked closer, there was not one trace of a fire, only the smell, sand, and ashes having piled up on the windowsills and gone inside. So we started the cleanup right away after we removed the sheets and the curtains to wash.

The end of November, my neighbor told me that their insurance company was having their entire house cleaned because of the smoke damage. This would be really nice for ours too, especially since it was up for sale, and the smoke damage was still there. But I did not want to make a claim, figuring the smell would evaporate eventually.

A week later, two men came to my door and showed their IDs that they were with my insurance company. Letting them in, I asked about their intentions, and they explained that they were cleaning fifty-seven homes in my neighborhood, and mine was one of them. They looked in all the rooms and talked with each other while doing so and finally returned to the living room.

They then informed me that if I agreed, their company would have my house cleaned, shampooed, and painted to get rid of the smoke odors. We informed them that we already cleaned up all the sand and ashes and the curtains and our clothes, but I would be grateful if they did the rest of what they offered.

They said a refund check would be coming in the amount it would have cost them to hire someone to do that clean up. The next day, their men arrived and shampooed the carpet and upholstery, and they said the painters would be here the day after. We were praising the Lord for all this because the house was even more perfect and clean now.

Our Christmas was very special because of God's special gift, His only begotten Son, our Savior. Stephen and Billy would be picked up for an afternoon with their dad and his girlfriend. They planned to tell their father one more time about this God who loved him and died for his sins.

When the boys were dropped off, they came back with presents, but what they wanted most did not happen. Assuring them that if we kept on praying daily for him that our merciful God would answer those prayers in His own perfect time, and we agreed to wait on our Lord.

Trip to Colorado

When my daughters were married, my sons and I wanted so much to move up to the mountains. Some friends from work had gone on vacation to Colorado and brought back lots of stories and pictures. When they told how beautiful it is and about the awesome mountains, that was all the boys and I talked about now.

We had been in love with Running Springs about five years before this Colorado idea came up. We went almost every weekend up to Running Springs and found some nice spot to have a picnic and play games. However, we wanted to actually live up there.

Now, we wanted to see if the Lord wanted us to live in the Colorado mountains. After some prayer and talks with family and friends, the boys and I decided to keep the house on the market and see what God would do.

In wanting to live in Colorado so much, I talked with my supervisor, Barney Doud, and my director, Paul Eshelman, about it at one of our breaks. Paul said that the most exiting way to live this Christian life is on the edge of faith. Encouraging me to move forward because God would close the door if it was not the right plan, my superiors wrote me some wonderful recommendations.

I sent résumés to seven of the Christian organizations that have their headquarters in Colorado Springs. One day, I got a phone call, and the person on the phone said, "This is the assistant of the Nick Cruz Ministry in Colorado Springs. My staff and I have gone over all the applications. We all agreed that we would like to have you join our staff here. When can you come?"

Bewildered, I laid the phone down and asked my supervisor who Nicky Cruz is, and he gave me a great description. Realizing that my boys and nephews had read and loved the books about Nick Cruz, I was excited. Barney figured the best time to go would be on the Easter vacation.

In one week, the boys would be out of school, and our office would be closed part of that time. The secretary agreed with me about the time to come and interview. We were praying for the will of God that evening, suddenly realizing that there was no way my car would make it to Colorado.

So by faith, I went to a car dealer the next day to see what they could do for me because to rent a motor home was way too much for me. The car dealer said that it would be a much lower payment to buy it. So my credit being very low, not thinking this possible, the Lord would have to take it in His hands.

After some time, he came back and said it is mine and to follow him to the office to sign the papers. He said the lowest down payment would be $400 and if I could bring that as soon as possible. My plan was to ask for half from my sister and half as an advance from my paycheck.

The man came back with the right price and payment, so now we owned a five-year-old, beautiful Dodge Mobile Traveler for $17,000. They would wait for the $400 down, and the first payment would be in one month.

It slept comfortably and had a 350 Dodge engine that purred like a kitten. Driving home to pick up Chris so she can drive my car back, it felt like this was a dream. Chris's mouth fell open when she saw the motor home; like me, she never imagined this possible.

The husband of my daughter Chris's said that she and the baby could come with us. There was no reason not to take them, and we saw later that this, too, was God's planning for us. So off we went after the Easter Sunday morning service and after saying farewell to our family.

We were full of excitement and had a big sign on the back that Chris had made: *Colorado or bust.* I still did not feel good about borrowing the down because part of the sign that this was from the Lord was that the money would be provided by Him.

Two days before we were to leave, there came a letter from my insurance company, and we thought it would be about the $250. This was because we had done our own cleanup after the panorama fire. Opening the letter and doing a double take, I called Chris to see if this could be true.

Then it was her turn to be shocked because the check was for $1,060.00—much more than we had expected. My gratefulness was overwhelming because now it would not be needful to borrow any money. The most wonderful reason of all was that we now had our final okay from our heavenly Father to take that Colorado trip.

So we loaded up our motor home with plenty of food and the bedding needed. We even found a wooden sign with my favorite verse on it, just like the big one over our front door: *As for me and my house, we will serve the Lord.*

After we had gone over everything one more time, we said a good night prayer, hoping for some good sleep. We would leave the next day early. It was also from the Lord that Chris came with us to Colorado. That 350 Dodge engine put me to sleep every half hour, and she had to do most of the driving.

There had never been time or money to take my kids on any kind of a trip, so that made this trip very special. After one more prayer for safety and good directions, we were ready to go. Being in this motor home was so much fun; we did not even want to get out to eat, but either cooked or bought, we could just eat inside.

We totally enjoyed beautiful Arizona, and the weather was absolutely perfect. Everyone we met stated this was the mildest spring weather they had seen in years. As we drove through the desert part of Arizona, there was the reason why the Lord had sent Chris along. My falling asleep every thirty minutes needed Chris to take over for me, and I was grateful to her.

Never having been to Arizona, it was unbelievable. One time, it was a desert, and an hour later, it was beautiful pine forests and snow-covered mountains. Our first night stop was in Flagstaff, and we were not sure we wanted to move on or just find a job and stay right there. But we moved on, and in the evening found our first KOA campground.

These campgrounds were strategically placed throughout the US and would always come up at dusk. They had showers, laundry rooms, electricity, and everything needed for safety. It was the most unbelievable trip and will stay forever on our minds.

We took lots of pictures with the camera the Lord had given us for this trip and enjoyed the great varieties of scenes, from the mountain ranges to the mysterious red cliffs. We never lost our way or ran out of food, water, or gasoline, and neither did our motor home overheat on those mountain ranges, thanks to our loving God.

We had spent our last night in Santa Fe and started out in the morning fog, but when we came to Colorado Springs, the sky opened up, and the sun came out as if the Lord wanted to welcome us. We stayed in the trailer park with the view directly of Pikes Peak for five dollars a night.

The next morning, Chris dropped me in front of the Nicky Cruz ministry, and while I had my interview, they went and had breakfast. It was a joy to meet the believers who were the staff of the Nicky Cruz Ministry; you could feel the loving Spirit there.

While the interview was going on, she realized that I did not come to stay but only for the interview. Being sure of having told them, I let them know that my house had not sold yet. They said they could give me one and a half months before they would have to find someone from their area.

There was one thing, however, we were disappointed about. We would not be able to live in the mountains because there were no villages to live in. The only one was Estes Park, and that was a two-and-a-half-hour, one-way drive from Running Springs. Our excitement about Colorado greatly diminished because we lived in the valley now.

On the weekends, we would go up to the San Bernardo Mountains because we loved the pine trees and mountain air so much. We would just have to see what God's will was in all this, and so we left Colorado, taking Route 70 home across the Rockies. We saw unbelievable beauty with breathtaking mountain ranges.

After we got back home, we needed to sell our wonderful mobile traveler; and advertising it, the first couple that came took it for a test drive with their little five-year-old girl, Angie. It was necessary for me to receive the money of the purchase because the full amount minus the $400 down was still due on it.

The couple and their daughter came back after a while and stated they would take it for the full price. They began to share with us why they knew it was theirs because God showed them. They did not realize that neither of them had paid attention to lock at the side door of the rig.

Their little girl was leaning against the door, and at a sharp curve, the door flew open, and Angie was thrown into the very busy street. It was after-work hour, and the cars swerved all around her, but not one touched her.

Before they could stop the vehicle and get out, Angie had already gotten up and came crying toward them, unhurt, only scared. They said they knew this was the Lord showing them the mobile home was theirs, and they wanted to pay the full price. We praised God!

The move to Running Springs

The Nicky Cruz Ministry finally had to call to notify me that they couldn't wait any longer and had to hire someone in Colorado Springs. We accepted it as the Lord's answer for that move and started looking in our San Bernardo Mountains for a home.

We wondered why the Lord let us go and see Colorado, and we realized if we had not seen ourselves that we could not live in the mountains there, we would have talked forever about Colorado and not truly appreciated what God had really planned for us.

My daughters were married and had their own homes to live in, and we saw them once or twice a week for dinner, mostly on Sundays. We still loved to have fun at the park, especially now that they had little ones themselves, and I loved getting to know them.

Our agent found a newly built A-frame in Running Springs with a furnished laundry room, a big beautiful stone fireplace, and a loft that the boys would enjoy. The home was in a lovely area close to where the boys would be picked up by the school buses and near three Campus Crusade staff, with whom I could daily carpool down to work.

This caused us to pray even harder for our own home to sell now that we had found this lovely home in Running Springs. The following day, a close friend who was our Realtor, brought us a family to look at our home.

They fell in love with it, bought it that day, and we started the paperwork on it. The escrow lasted seven days, and the next weekend, our family moved us up to Running Springs in the local mountains. We enjoyed those two years there so much and had found the most wonderful church with a youth group like AWANA.

Once again, my sons joined, and I became a leader for the girls. However, the winters at seven thousand feet were just too hard for a single mom. Many mornings I came out of the house and yelled, "Boys, where is my car?" It had snowed heavy all day and all night, and my car was totally covered.

Having lost two of my car pool friends made coming to work hard because the third one worked only three days a week. So we prayed for wisdom, and our faithful Lord showed us once again how and where, but in the most unexpected way.

The people who had bought our house divorced, so they were not able to pay the balance they owed me on the house. A friend's husband working at Campus Crusade came to me with the most unusual offer.

He knew about my wanting to live in the mountains, and he and his wife lived in Crestline. They had two houses there, and it was only 5,500 feet high and was much easier to access and depart than our former location. The houses were side by side on a mountain outside the city, and they were planning to rent one of them.

He offered to buy my house from the people, and for the balance they owed me, he would be willing to let the boys and me live in the house next to them, rent-free for five years. We were so thrilled and amazed, agreeing that our future home was a gift from our heavenly Father.

The house had two big bedrooms, an awesome view, and a perfect deck for me to do my oil painting. Those five years were some of the most joyful of our lives, and to this day, we talk about them and see it whenever we are up there.

Well, I didn't have to leave my beloved mountains until Stephen and then Billy went into the service, and it was too hard for me to live up there alone. Coming down very sad, I rented a room from a friend, which, once again, turned out to be part of God's perfect plan for me. There were special times with the God I loved and saw parts of Him that were new to me.

Also, there was now much more time for me to be in the ministries the Lord had given me, of which two of the facilities were only five minutes away from my new home. Of course, I still had my full-time job with my beloved Jesus Film Project. It became visible to me that He always causes us to grow as He knows it is for our best.

Billy's healing

Billy had grown four more inches now, and it was time for another surgery to extend the shunt in his neck. The doctor ordered the same x-rays and tests as before, except this time, he continued the tests two more times, then was gone a while. When he finally returned, he sat down and said calmly, "I guess you won't have to see me again."

Seeing my surprised look, the doctor explained that Billy won't ever need a surgery again. He continued saying that he has only seen this one time before in his long practice, but Billy's own shunt had opened and is draining the fluid into his heart by itself.

The doctor told me if I have $2,800, he can take the artificial shunt out, but it would be fine leaving it in; Billy will have no problems. Well we thanked the Lord with all our hearts and had a nice dinner and his favorite ice cream.

My daughters' relationships with their husbands were still not good, and their emotions changed from day to day. It was obvious there was no trust between the partners because they had no confidence in themselves and were not able to trust each other or God.

Knowing that my Lord and Savior was capable and willing to change that, my prayers were daily for this to happen and that it would be soon, for their own and their children's happiness.

They also could not see the changes in my life yet; we hardly ever saw each other in these times. Even though the Lord saved me from drinking and dating, my control over anger was not fixed yet. So when we saw each other, we argued about the things that had not changed in our lives, and we just could not leave the past alone yet.

However, their fights with their spouses were less often and less hateful, and the Lord taught me to trust Him about this. He reminded me that as He was patient with me; now it was time for me to do the same for them. The Lord waited for thirty-seven years for me to answer His call on my life and let Him make me into someone usable.

Another hip surgery

There were some problems with my right hip again, and it was necessary for another surgery. The pain had been so bad I could hardly walk upright for a while. My family, as well as friends, had told me to go and see my orthopedist who knew me well from previous times.

After a few x-rays, he informed me that the artificial part of the hip had broken away from the real bones again. The doctor needed more tests before surgery, and he said one of them would be painful, but there could not be anesthesia.

My friends and church prayed for me, and never before was His presence so real. Feeling just bathed in His grace and love, many scriptures flowed through my mind. Both the doctor and the nurse told me that I was the best patient they ever had for this procedure.

Two days later, my mom dropped me at the hospital and went back to my house to take care of the boys and be there for my four-week recuperation. Sitting in the registration room, I was completely calm; there was no fear this time.

After sign in and getting my bracelet put on, they took me to my room. Stretching out in bed, I noticed a young woman in the only other bed in the room. Asking my Savior to give me someone to tell all about Him and His great love, I knew He would.

Roommate Lucy

Dinner was being served just then, and this was a good time to start a conversation. After introducing myself, I asked her the reason for being here. She told me her name was Lucy and that due to an accident, she was here for one of the many surgeries to get her walking again. There seemed to be an immediate bond, and I thanked my Lord.

My operation was scheduled for the next morning; that gave me a chance to tell Lucy that there is no fear of tomorrow's surgery. Sharing that it was because God was there every moment in the past, she listened intently. While falling asleep, I thanked the Lord for having me here at this time for a special reason.

My heart was at rest, knowing that all was well at home with both Lita and Chris helping my mom with the boys. At the hospital, everything ran smoothly. My doctor commented that my surgery went unusually well.

There was less pain than before, which meant I could get up sooner and would be home earlier than the past times. Coming back to my room, Lucy had her family visiting; and a friend came to see me, so our conversation would continue tomorrow.

My visiting friend apologized for not coming to see me earlier and handed me a gift and a card. I told her that the Lord may have wanted her to come late so we could talk for a while. This must have hit the nail on the head because she started to cry and told me that there were problems in her marriage.

Reaching for my Bible, I began to look for scriptures that were just right for her need. The right verses were able to assure her that God would make things right between her and her husband. If she were willing to be used by the Holy Spirit in her husband's, life there was no telling what wonderful and exciting things will happen.

It was a real victory for Jesus to see her walking away with a smile and believe that the Lord is in control because she was His. The next day, I had quite a few visitors, so I did not get to say much to my roommate; but I was sure my Father would give me time with her, knowing by now that the Holy Spirit had to do His softening work in the heart first.

So I was willing to wait until it was the right time. That evening, another friend stopped by and confided in me the trouble she was having with her kids. With real gratefulness, I realized for the first time that the women the Lord had brought to me so far all had trouble with their husbands, but mostly with their children.

This was not due to my being a good example of a lasting marriage, but because what they had been through were my experiences also. Being able to show them the only answer there is in this dark and lost world is Jesus Christ gives them hope. Wanting to serve my Savior more than anything, it was a blessing to be a tool for Him in some way.

Sharing the faithful work He did with my children in spite of my mistakes showed me why He could use me. He wanted me to encourage people who are in trouble or hurting with the same comfort and love with which He has comforted me.

This told me that my beloved Savior had brought me out of my afflictions to help those who find themselves in the same situation. This knowledge made me fall even deeper in love with Him, and to know that He can use me made my heart rejoice. We were truly encouraged to see that there is no subject that is not covered in God's Word.

The next evening, after the dinner dishes had been picked up and we had no visitors, I did not feel like watching TV but felt like dwelling on the events of the last two days. Lucy saying she did not want to watch the boob tube either made this the right time.

With a tingle all over me, I began the conversation by telling her about my children, of which the two boys had come to visit me that afternoon. Sharing just a little about my hurtful past and how God in His love had pulled us out of it, her attention was on me.

Sharing a little more about some of the changes after this Savior had entered our lives, she listened closely. Telling her how, after pulling us out of the mire, He brought us into His family forever caused her to rise.

Gently I asked her if she would like to give her life to this God, who gave His beloved Son to die for her and her children. Lucy did not hesitate at all and repeated the salvation prayer after me, and I could tell that she meant it.

Revealing to her through Scripture that all the angels in heaven were rejoicing because she had come home, I could promise by experience that God would have His hand on her life from now, that He would also touch her children's hearts made her cry.

We closed our evening by reading my favorite part where He says, "You have loved Me. Therefore, I will deliver you. I will set you securely on high because you have known My name. You will call upon Me, and I will answer you. I will be with you in trouble. I will rescue you and honor you with a long life. I will satisfy you and let you behold My salvation."

By pointing out that God will not remove our troubles, but promises to be with us in them to make us stronger, she would not be discouraged when they don't just vanish.

This was not the end of our friendship. On Christmas, she came to visit me in my home with her family, and we talked about God's wonderful plan. Lucy had made me a lovely country basket with flowers on top, and I gave her a Living Bible.

Roommate Nancy

Getting out of bed was still not possible for me yet, but I was anxious to find out who was crying across the hall. Asking the nurse, she told me that it was a young lady named Nancy, who had broken her kneecap in a bad fall and was in pain.

That morning, the doctor told me that I can go into the wheelchair for half an hour after therapy. After having been brought back to my room, I wheeled myself into the room of the young lady with the injured knee. Her pretty tearstained face looked at me in surprise.

My question if I could help her seemed really strange, seeing the position we were both in, so we both giggled. She asked me to get a nurse because her bell had fallen off the bed, and neither of us were able to retrieve it.

The nurse had made her a little more comfortable, and so I stayed with her a while. Having introduced myself, she said her name is Nancy. Trying to cheer her up, I shared about my body cast. This was after my third hip surgery, and the cast started at my toes and ended under my chest.

She was laughing in no time as I made her visualize my itching everywhere. It was funny, telling of all the contraptions the orderlies and nurses' aides and even one doctor built to reach all the places I was itching. She was calm now and had stopped crying, so I asked for another visit the next day, and she agreed with a smile.

After therapy and lunch, they put me back into a wheelchair, and to my delight, Nancy was put in one also. She smiled at me and said, "Wanna race?" We rolled ourselves out to the visiting room, which had a very big window facing the backyard with a lovely view.

It was so good to feel the warmth of the sun and see that life on the outside went on as usual. We told each other about different parts of our lives, and I found out that Nancy had broken her kneecap at school. That happened in a fight with a rival and had not been the first disagreement between them.

She was one of the thousands of young women out there who come from a broken home. The only problem was that in this situation, they settle for the first guy that tells them that he loves them, and they will believe that. Sadly enough, this does not just happen to the young ones.

Her boyfriend abandoned her when he found out that she was pregnant, and then she lost the baby two weeks later. She did not want the boyfriend back and tried to make it on her own. My heart ached for her, and I wanted her to know my Savior's love. Telling Nancy about some of the hurt in my life and having been left with four children after fifteen years of marriage got her attention.

This made her more relaxed and at ease with me because I could relate to her. It encouraged me to tell her about the one who had healed all my bitterness and gave me something beautiful to look forward to. We talked a while more, but since we had two more days, I did not want to overwhelm her with all of His good news at once.

We were not allowed out of bed the rest of the day, so my rest was in God's Word until a few visitors came. The following day, we met by the big window in the visiting room, and no one else was there. Sharing about my daughters' unhappy past and God changing it caused her to really listen.

Being sure that my loving heavenly Father was working to turn their confusion into faith, we prayed for her and them.

Nancy was looking down on her hand, and I saw the tears fall. This gave me the courage to asked her if she wanted to know this God who loved her so much that He let His Son die for her sins in a terrible way. She nodded her head, and I asked if she wanted to pray after me, and she nodded again.

On that sunny afternoon, another sinner entered the kingdom of God, and I told her also about the angels rejoicing over her. Continuing to encourage her with Jesus's resurrection, which now had a great meaning to her, I told her that the Savior said, "Because I rose, you will rise also," and that included her now.

Nancy's grandma came to pick her up the next morning, and she wheeled into my room, handing me a piece of paper. She smiled and said "Thanks for everything" and left the hospital. When I opened the paper, she had drawn a rose on it and said "With love, Nancy" and had her address and phone number. I had given her mine earlier and told her we would stay in touch.

Roommate Diana

Well, I had a new roommate, and hers is the most unusual case I have ever heard or seen. She entered the room, carefully escorted by a doctor and an assistant, and was helped into bed in an unusual fashion. She was being harnessed into all kinds of equipment to hold her head very still and not be able to move in any way.

The doctor explained that if they had not found her at this time, she would have terrible complications and pain, plus a chance of never moving or walking again. After they left, we could introduce ourselves. She said her name was Diana and began to tell me her strange story.

She said she had been visiting a friend in another state and, driving with this friend, got in a car accident. After being treated for cuts and bruises, she was released with some pain pills. Being in pain, she took the pills and, after a few days, went back home to her husband and daughter.

Diana came down with a bad cold and went to see her doctor, and when she signed in, someone recognized her name from a report and told her doctor that she was being searched for. They sent an ambulance, and she was brought to the hospital where I was and signed into my room (total coincidence).

Diana was very self-sufficient and, within an hour or so, had everything arranged with her insurance. Then she notified her husband of her whereabouts and made arrangements with a person who would care of their ten-year-old daughter while her husband worked.

The next day, when things had settled down, she told me a little of her life and asked for my reason for being there. When she found out that I was a Christian, she said quietly and with sadness in her voice that she used to be one but backslid badly. Sharing a little of how the Lord had worked in mine and my children's lives brightened her face.

She was very quiet, and I assured her that God has never given up on her and is patiently waiting for her to come back to Him. We both got some visitors then, and I left the continuation of our talk to the Lord.

Chris informed me that things are going well at home, and the boys are keeping their quiet time. Every other day, they were having a Bible study, which really put my mind at ease.

The next day was hectic for Diana. She always had someone there, either for tests or for preparation for surgery. The nurse said that this lady had walked around with a broken neck for almost two weeks till they found her.

In the evening, however, it was still, when Diana's voice suddenly hit my ear. My therapy was more strenuous now, and I had been dozing but was wide-awake when I heard what she was saying. Softly crying, she said that she was scared and would I please pray with her.

Assuring her that God loved requests for help, and that He will be listening for our every word, we prayed together, and she told the Lord that she wanted to be His again. She was rededicating her life to Him, and I could tell she really meant it.

We were asking Him for a calm heart for her and a very steady hand for the surgeon in her operation the following day. In the morning, the noises woke me as she was being picked up. As she rolled by, I said, "Remember who is at your side every moment," and she smiled.

The next day, my doctor came in early and notified me that my healing was unusually fast, so my release would be six days early, and I can go home the following day. That morning, Diana was brought back with a hideous contraption around her neck and shoulders, making every move impossible for her.

She was wide-awake and was joking about her harness, that it would not keep her from talking even though she would have to lie still for a while. She said that everything went well, and she gave God the credit for the good outcome.

Before leaving the next morning, we talked some more about the new beginning of her life, and after a sisterly farewell and having each other's addresses, they wheeled me to my mom's car. Suddenly I realized with a heart full of love toward my Savior how many more sisters He had given me to spend eternity with.

Juvenile hall ministry

It was 1989, one year before Stephen would leave for the service and Billy would leave two years later, that my beloved Lord gave me a new ministry. Knowing I would be lost by their absence, He got me involved in the local juvenile hall youth prison.

The relationship with my two sons was closer than it would have been normally because our lives were more intimate. My daughters were gone from home for a while now, and I did not have a husband to spend half of my time with. So my life was always the boys and I, and almost everything we did, we did together.

However, my beloved God knew of the painful time to come and had already planned ahead. The chaplain of the local Juvenile Hall ministry had invited me to join the Spiritual Concerns Committee and represent Campus Crusade for Christ, which made me joyfully accept.

When one of the Bible teachers was moving away, he challenged me to take over his unit. Having heard things about it, my answer was a careful "I will give it a try." After some training, going through the background check and finger printing, we met at juvenile hall.

When they locked the fifth door behind us, it became real that there would be no quick escape. Being a little nervous when entering the unit he was assigned to, my faith took over, keeping me calm. There was a long corridor having steel doors with small windows and young faces looking out behind them.

In the middle of the room were benches and tables, and we sat down. The staff would release each of the young inmates, one cell at a time, asking them if they wanted to attend Bible study. To my surprise, all agreed and began to sit down on the benches in irregular order because there were members of different gangs in the unit.

Finding myself strangely drawn to the young faces, I watched in amazement how they were attentive to the teaching, and many had questions about the lesson. The Bible teacher asked me to answer some of the questions, and seeing their faces on me was truly moving.

After that night's lesson, two of the boys came up to me and asked, "Would you come back next week?" And when I answered "You bet," their faces lit up. The teacher said that this was his last night before he moved and that he felt very confident about my taking over the unit and told the chaplain in charge that I could be trusted to be his replacement.

There were a few months of training ahead and more of checking my background. Awaiting the first day in my assigned unit, I prayed and studied for a lesson, knowing the teaching would be to young people of whom some had never read the Bible. Quite a few did not know how to read, so I never assigned a reader but always asked for a volunteer.

This took a different approach to God's Word, and it was needful to explain seldom used words. The staff had given me an extra half hour after the Bible lesson to pray with the youths one on one. That was when I heard their private heartaches and rejections from their families.

The probation department gave me permission for the young people to write their names and prayer requests in my notebook. One of the purposes was for me to be able to pray for them every day. Whenever one of the young prisoners prayed to receive Jesus as his Savior and Lord, I asked them to draw a cross next to their name.

As Bible teachers left, I was asked to give studies in more than one unit a week. My prayers had to be by the page now instead of by name. A second book was needed, and by the time I left for San Clement six years later, there were 6,104 prayers for salvation in the books, and I still have them.

Before leaving each Bible study, I promised my youth that I would come looking for them when entering heaven. They were pleased and surprised that I was sure they would be there, and I repeated God's promises on this subject.

My children's dad saved

One week before Stephen left for the Army, he told me that Billy and him wanted to take Dad fishing in his wheelchair. They planned to take him to Glen Helen Park, which had a lake with fishing privileges and wheelchair abilities.

Their plan was to witness to their dad one more time. Stephen wanted to know if anything happened, he would see his dad again. So they told Bill about the fishing plan, and on a Wednesday, went to pick him up.

It was two hours later that I received the awaited call where Stephen said, "Mom, the kingdom of God has a new member." Our longtime fervent prayer was answered in God's own perfect timing. Praise to His holy name.

Here was another reason for our faith to grow and a way to encourage others to keep praying for the salvation of those they care about. Our God loves those kinds of prayers, and He will answer if we trust Him to do it.

Stephen's enlistment

As expected, even though I tried not to think about it, Stephen joined the Army and was swished away before he got to enjoy his graduation. We lived in the mountains and because of "snow days," graduation was postponed, but the Army could not wait. He had asked us to call him Steve now that he was grown-up, and we did.

Long before Steve left, I began to pray fervently, asking our Savior to please have his roommate be a Christian.

After he was settled in, he called me and excitedly told me that the young soldier he roomed with knew the Lord, and the two of them would attend church services on Sundays.

His letters came two or three times a week, and in one of them, he shared a great story, showing how his faithful God was taking care of him. Ha and his roommate went out one Saturday evening in his friend's car to play pool at the PX, which was something the two of them liked to do.

After several hours, his buddy had befriended a girl, and a short time after, she persuaded his friend to come home with her. Steve watched them walk away with her holding on tightly to his friend. So he sat down on the curb, knowing he had no ride back, and he began to pray.

He asked the Lord to make his buddy realize the girl's intentions and cause him to come back. Suddenly, when already down the street, Steve's buddy took the girl's arms off himself and started walking back to him and said, "Let's go." My son said that he gratefully thanked the Lord for answering his prayer.

While Steve was stationed in Colorado, I had the chance to visit him for a week, two times a year, and got to stay with some of the Campus Crusade staff living and working there. Knowing these people from working together at Arrowhead Springs, it was great to be with them again.

They had my son over for a meal and church on Sundays and Wednesdays and sometimes in between. My faithful God had answered my prayer to have His hand on my child. Realizing that the Lord would take care of what I give Him, my trust in Him grew deeper.

Billy's enlistment

Two years later, Billy graduated from the same school as Steve did and we got to enjoy his celebration. However, it was bittersweet for me because he had signed up for the California Conservation Corps because he loved the outdoors and often worked with carving things out of wood; that is what he chose.

He became a firefighter, and I got many letters and pictures from those years. Billy had also asked us to call him Bill now, and we did. The pictures are a cute remembrance because his hair was long then, and he looked like a logger.

Once again, this mother pleaded with God to let him have a Christian friend that would not lead him down the wrong road. On one of the work days, Bill's team and their leader, David, were to take out an unusually large tree trunk.

While working, Bill saw his boss's name tag and said to him, "My sister has the same last name as you." His superior looked at Bill's name tag and said, "Oh, my sister-in-law had the same last name as you." Laughingly, they realized that they were related because Bill's sister and David's brother were married.

David was the only Christian in his very large family, and this dear man and his wife made Bill as one of their own and had him at their house and in church as much as possible. Bill came to love David because he treated him like his own son.

My heart was so grateful to my God because once again, He had answered this mother's prayer for my son's protection. Every three or four month I would drive up to visit my son in Northern California and had a chance to meet David and his sweet family. Staying at their home, we came to love each other, and we are still friends today.

I had given a fourth one of my children into the hand of God when leaving home and trusted Him to keep His hand on him. How could I not love this awesome Lord with all my heart when He kept proving Himself so faithful?

Move to San Clemente

In 1993, the Jesus Film Project, which I had been a part of, was only half of the project located on the Arrowhead Springs grounds. The other half was located in Laguna Niguel, and the leadership wanted us to be united. They found the perfect building to house us all in San Clemente, a beautiful city on the Pacific Ocean.

God impressed on me strongly to move to San Clemente with my office, and I obeyed, even though it was very hard for me to leave my big family. That family of mine by now existed of four children and their mates, eight grandchildren and their mates, and by then, fourteen great-grandchildren.

A friend found me a lovely apartment with an ocean view, but on the weekends, my heart drew me to San Bernardino. The mountains were always my first love, so we spent much time up there because we have always enjoyed the outdoors and love camping.

However, the last five years before moving to the beach, I got violently ill when it was very hot. The doctor told me it was called heatstrokes, and one of them would be my last one. However, living at the beach, my time could be spent outside in the daytime without ever getting sick.

One weekend, when I left San Bernardino to go back to San Clemente, I was crying and told the Lord that it was hard to leave my family. He answered, "Hannah, have I not given you the best of both places?"

I was very ashamed and thanked Him for His love with all my heart. The Lord allowed me to buy a lovely mobile home near the beach, and now my family could also come here sometimes.

As soon as possible, after some more training, my ministry could continue by volunteering at the juvenile hall in the city of Orange; this center was four times bigger than the one in San Bernardino. Even though it was a one-and-a-half-hour drive each week, I enjoyed teaching God's Word and was grateful for Him using me to lead so many to his Son Jesus Christ.

Camp Pendleton Marine Base

About that time, one of my grandsons, Chris's son, joined the Marines and, after boot camp, was stationed at Camp Pendleton Marine Base next to San Clemente. My visits to him were about three or four times a week, and we would sit in my van or on a picnic table and have snacks and Bible studies. Soon two or three of his buddies would join us, which made me ask the Lord to send even more of the young marines.

Longing to do this more often and on a larger scale caused me to inquire who was staffing this base with religious volunteers and found out it was the navigators. Calling their headquarters in Colorado Springs, I got the name and number of the man and set up an appointment to meet with him.

Mentioning my longtime connection with Campus Crusade for Christ, he was delighted and explained that they had a couple from Campus Crusade leading the Bible studies. They were there for five years but then were transferred overseas. He said the only negative thing was that there was only a Quonset hut available, which was hot in the summer and cold in the winter.

Remembering a building when meeting with my grandson, which had a big YMCA sign on it, and contacting the base, I found out the name of the local director for this organization and made an appointment. Presenting my permission to meet with marines, I asked if I could be allowed to use their facilities for Bible studies; and to my great joy, they agreed to it.

My announcements were placed on the different poster boards, and only seven came on the first night. These seven pleaded with me to give them a second time in the week, and asking the YMCA leaders, I was allowed to do so. Well, guess what? On the second night, there were fifteen marines who asked me to give them a third night of Bible study, and once again, the okay was given.

The numbers of attendees increased to anywhere from fifteen to thirty a night, depending on the companies that were in from the field training. The young marines asked for more days of studies, but the rest of the days, the YMCA had their own programs, and we had to keep it to three days a week, three hours a night.

This began the most joyful of my ministries because those of my Bible study soldiers, who were off on the weekend, could come home with me. I would pick them up on Friday evening and return them to base on Sunday nights.

That way, they would not be tempted to go to the big city with their unbelieving roommates, where the drugs were cheap and so were the girls. Instead, we went to shows, church programs, or barbecued at the beautiful beach by the San Clemente pier. The pictures of those days were many and a joy to me.

At those times, there were good opportunities to pray with them one on one and get to know the joys and pains about their families, especially girlfriends. Many of them joined the Marine Corps to get away from their family or to help out their single mom.

One of my marines was notified that his dad was in a fight and got killed. He got a week leave to go home and be with his family. He came back heartbroken because his mom was such a mess he did not even get to talk with her.

Making sure there was extra time for me to spend with him, he had a chance to pour out his heart. Once again I could tell him of God's deep and endless love for him. He told me how grateful he was for my being there for him as well as the others who were hurting, but I told him that the thanks go only to God who had sent me there.

The Lord began healing him, and we had other chances to talk. We prayed together often till it was time for him to leave for home. He wrote me an awesome farewell letter, as did most of my spiritual sons when they left this base. Having stacks of them, whenever Satan tries to get me down, I take them out and read a few to him, and he gives up.

On Sundays, we would attended my church and have lunch at our favorite restaurant at the harbor, and I have many pictures of these times. There are also pictures of my spiritual sons spread out all over my couches and floors, wrapped in sleeping bags, spending Friday and Saturday nights.

I was loving this more than juvenile hall was because I could teach my young inmates and even see them on the visiting day, but I always had to leave them there. The most precious times to me were all the chances for counseling and prayer for them to receive Christ.

Never would I have ever imagined all this when I first surrendered my life to the Lord my God. These young men—I had thousands of them—said I was their spiritual mom, and so they all called me Mom, which helped me greatly with missing my own faraway sons. This was, once again, the way my beloved Savior showed His love.

There were snacks at the Bible study break time, and many of them wanted me to pray for them then or after the study. The YMCA room had an enormously big TV, and whenever I had new soldiers in my group, because of other companies arriving, I would show the Campus Crusade Jesus film, which they truly enjoyed.

A few times, some of my guys had to go overseas and were stationed in war zones, which caused the rest of us to do some serious praying. When these young men returned, we were all so grateful because they reported of total safety to all in their company. They shared that not one of their buddies were injured or killed.

Given the opportunity at the start of each Bible study for the invitation to receive Jesus as their Lord and Savior was most important to me. The notebooks I started so my marines could write their names and prayer requests in were full in no time.

Those books were, and still are, my most valuable possession. As some of my marines left or were released, they wrote me letters, saying how much they thanked God for having me there for them. They loved to hear about the awesome love of God and that He promised never to leave or forsake them.

These precious names and prayer requests I shared with my family and friends and, most of all, my supporters. We prayed for those requests many times, and I found out over the years that so many of these requests our beloved Lord answered.

It is a joy for me to still be in touch with some of my marines and hear that they are happily married and have children. They still spend much of their time in the Word of God, and we stay in touch.

Return to San Bernardino

My love for the Jesus film was still very strong, yet at the end of ten years in San Clemente, the Lord clearly showed me to return to San Bernardino. I would truly miss my Jesus Film Project coworkers, especially my best friend, Sharon.

We became close friends in 1993 when we both worked with the film in the same office in San Clemente. She is also a popular country singer, and when possible, I go down to spend a day or two with her and go with her to one of her performances when possible.

By His clear leading, I ended up with our Chinese ministries for almost ten years. Trying to call the human resources for info, by chance, Dr. David Hock Ta answered the phone, stating he was the director for the Chinese ministry. Explaining that my job is a finance developer, and I needed to come back to San Bernardino, he got excited.

He said that the Chinese ministry had been praying for a finance developer for a while and if I would take the job. Being aware that this was of the Lord, I agreed, and this started a wonderful working and personal relationship with him and his wife.

Dr. Tey's son, Moses, and his family joined him in this ministry, and we had some wonderful volunteers come to help us as well. Dr. Tey had written ten books by then, which were also translated into Chinese. The work with more than two hundred Chinese churches in Los Angeles brought great joy, blessings, and awesome results.

After many great years of working with them, they gave up the office in San Bernardino. Dr. Hock Tey and his son, Moses, were doing their powerful ministry four times a year in the Government-approved churches in China. So once again, I asked the Lord to show me what is next.

Knowing my love for the Jesus film, the Lord had already a plan. One day, I got a call from Vance Nordman, the head of the Jesus DVD Project. He said he would like me to work for him and added that I could stay where I lived and do the work from my home, as he and his whole team were doing.

His department is called Reaching the Nations Among Us, an exciting, well-planned outreach. Working with the immigrants is a blessing because we have the Jesus film now in 1,500 languages, which gives us an open door. As of March 2018, we have sent out almost five million DVDs and are praising God for this great success.

Knowing Vance and his wife from my ten years in San Clemente, this was a great answer. I would be with my beloved Jesus film again, yet my work would be from home, and I can stay with my family and my ministries. How could I ever thank my Savior for the way He always arranges my life to give me joy?

Additional youth

While living in San Clement and visiting weekends in San Bernardino, my son Bill asked me to visit his church. When the leadership at his church found out how many years I had taught young people, the youth pastor asked if I could help him.

He was trying to start a high school group but had no one to help yet. So he asked me if I would be willing to assist him and teach them every other Sunday till it ran well, and I agreed. I was willing to do it for seven months, being anxious to get back to my own church, which is Immanuel Baptist.

Some of the senior youth in Bill's church, especially five of them, wanted more than just every other Sunday and asked if I could teach them one evening a week at my house. That sounded great, and I asked them how many of them had invited Jesus into their life and how many got baptized. They admitted that none of them had done either.

They prayed to receive the Lord with me the following Sunday morning, and I had several hours to explain the meaning of baptism from the Bible. The youth pastor agreed to theirs and others' baptism the same afternoon in a member's pool, and we were just rejoicing. He also asked if I would like to baptize my five youth myself to which they and I happily agreed.

A church picnic had been arranged for that afternoon, and a time was planned for sharing something God had done in anyone's life. To my great surprise, David, one of my students, stood up and agreed to tell his news. Boldly and loudly he proclaimed that he had received Jesus as his Lord and Savior this morning, and he got baptized this day and wanted to follow God from now on.

This was the most joyful day for me and my precious students, and we truly celebrated. They not only continued to come for my Monday evening Bible classes but began to bring their friends and their girlfriends for the study, who then also gave their lives to the Savior.

One thing I had to be very careful of was never ever taking credit for this success as my doing. It scared me because it would be easy to give Satan that chance. Mentioning to my precious Savior that if there would be any pride sneaking in, I would drop it all like a hot potato, truly meaning that.

We all loved the verse that He would finish the work that He had begun in them so there was no reason for me to get anxious. Teaching this was important so they would not get discouraged when things would not change as fast as they wanted it to.

These precious new believers needed to be encouraged and praised for any progress. All of them are married and in good jobs now, and one of them has been in seminary and is ready to graduate and become a pastor.

The Potter's vessels

The thing I loved teaching most of all, besides assurance of salvation, was becoming now that vessel God had planned for them to be. It would have to be a vessel that He could use in the lives of others. The reason this was so dear to me is because of my resembling so very little the piece of yielding clay I wanted to be for my Savior.

The old me was so self-sufficient and opinionated most of my life I would have been better compared with a rubber ball. Belonging now to that creative and imaginative Potter, I longed to be worked into something pleasing to Him. That meant whichever way He would choose to knead, press, or stretch, there would be no complaints or grumbling from me.

This also meant holding still whether He showered me with blessings or left me on the shelf to dry and do without for a while. It was easy for me to praise Him when His working was visible. However, when trouble came along, I still searched first if there was any way I could solve it myself before surrendering.

However, as soon as I remembered and accepted that this was part of my refining process, it became easier to hold still to His work in me. Even now, my acceptance is not instant yet, but He taught me that all clay has to do is lay still and trust the Potter to do His precious work of shaping and molding.

Yet when He really began to make this piece pliable, I would still squirm and resist, but that happened less and less often. It became clear to me that I must be totally surrendered, trusting in His promises.

That promise is to make me into a vessel that He can use and bring honor to Him. The resources the world had to offer were never what they seemed, and realizing that, I ran back into my Father's loving hands. Even though He forgave me when I confessed, He did not always remove the consequences of my actions.

Sixteen of my family members and a few of their friends had followed me into the kingdom by now, and that was a miracle. Starting to pray with even more fervor for the rest of them to come to know the Lord and fall in love with Him, it began to happen. He always answers these kind of prayers.

Not being able to teach my daughters how to have a lasting marriage, I shared with them the difference God would have made had my husband and I let Him be the center in our lives, showing them the only way their marriages would work is if they accept His rules because He knows our characters so well.

He also does not leave us alone to keep these rules. He gave us the Holy Spirit, in whose power we can obey. The Father knows us so very intimately and always considers our human weaknesses. Revealing from scriptures, I showed them that all He wants is our love and obedience, then He can send His blessings and perfect what is still weak in us.

He promises me that when I am weak, then He can use His strength. Knowing this earlier would have really helped me. There are so many good books out on marriage and child raising. Getting one for each of my girls, I prayed that the Holy Spirit would give them a hunger to use the great advice.

My Monday evening Bible studies continued, and there were nine senior students by now, and I used the teaching of the Potter and the clay often. When we messed up, I had to place these vessels, including myself, back in the Potter's hands, reminding myself that I was only to teach them of

His ways and not to take control over their minds (thank God).

It was the Lord's responsibility to make them what He had wanted them to be, and He took care of their growth. He would use me to teach them His awesome word and thousands of promises; my part was then to stand back, pray, and enjoy. Once I recognized that and believe it, there was a new freedom and joy in me while teaching all these young people.

His technique in bringing this about was almost always different from I would have used, and it did not take me long to bow to His precious will. The very best thing I could do was keep them in my daily prayers, as I did for my own family.

It was very important to never give up, no matter how it looked in my eyes. Only if the Potter does His skillful work will we become that honorable vessel that he can use for those who seek Him.

In time, I learned that my old sinful nature, which has been saved, now needs to be transformed by the renewing of my mind according to Romans 12:1–2. This continues every time I'm in His precious word, and the guilt trips Satan tried to lay on me became less often. Now I could enter the battle wearing the full armor of our Redeemer, which needs to be put on daily.

The only time we would suffer defeat was when we laid down the spiritual weapons and tried it in our own strength, and the old nature would temporarily come to the surface. Explaining that we must daily take up the Sword of the Spirit, which is the Word of God, and cut off its ugly head finally began to help.

It was a true joy to me as these precious young people kept growing, and they now attended a very popular, Bible teaching church closer to their homes. This all encouraged me to never give up on any young person, no matter how they were when they first entered my life or how little they knew about God at that time.

Trip to Russia

After being with my beloved Campus Crusade for Christ for sixteen years, my children being gone from home and having started their own lives, the Lord allowed me to travel. Going to other countries was a dream come true, and my live became an unbelievable adventure.

The first opportunity was a convocation trip to Russia to meet with teachers to share with them how they could teach the life and the message of God to their students. They had not been allowed to even speak about God for seventy years, and things had changed.

The country's minister of education contacted the Jesus film department and asked if we could put together a curriculum with which to train the teachers and leave it with them so they can use it for their classes. We were excited and ready in no time.

It was an indescribable feeling to stand on a hill in Moscow, overlooking the city that we had heard so much about for years. We learned to know the Russian people to be kind and generous. We met many who once were in high and responsible positions now taking their poverty with a great amount of grace.

We started out with a very unusual twenty-hour ride on a train terribly overheated. The windows were nailed shut so no one could open them to cool down. Local passengers who took the train often said that it was usually very, very cold.

However, when it was known that fourteen Americans were coming, they tried to keep us nice and hot for twenty hours of the ride. We had four at each cabin at night and doubled up for the study time. We laughed and acknowledged what *togetherness* means.

Needless to say, we did not use the wool blankets given us, but we enjoyed the flavorful tea in their beautiful silver and glass mugs and the tasty biscuits. Every day we had to meet and practice our daily lessons to be sure in presenting them accurately.

We met with the teachers of the first city assigned to us, and a little over four hundred of them were waiting for us. We were hesitant, not knowing what to expect, and we could see their shy attempts to politely greet us. However, it didn't take long before both groups discovered an affection for each other.

The Russians have a wonderful welcoming ceremony that their guests truly enjoy. There are usually six to seven Russian women dressed in their beautiful national costumes, one of them holding a white lace tablecloth. On that cloth is a tray with a braided loaf of bread and a small bowl of salt.

Every guest walks up in turn, breaks a piece of the bread, and dips it a little in the salt. As soon as the piece of bread was eaten, we were now considered friends. It was an emotional moment, and this was repeated each time we entered a new school.

The feeble attempts of both groups to get to know each other brought some laughter, and soon there was a feeling of camaraderie none of us expected. We had only heard of the other as enemies and admitted how totally human and natural we felt toward each other as we might for our neighbors at home.

Training sessions lasted every day from 4:00 p.m. to 8:00 p.m. but almost never ended before midnight. Each group of teachers got to see the Jesus film on the first evening. Tears flowed as lives were given to the Savior. Many of the schoolchildren would perform for us during the evening sessions in their lovely costumes, and most of the music were popular American songs.

In the mornings, the teachers invited their instructors to visit their class and watch them teach the lesson from the previous afternoon. It was awesome to see them teach Bible stories, and often the principal would also come and watch the performance.

One of the larger cities had planned our program, and we had studied well and were prepared for the 380 teachers waiting for us. Suddenly two of the school leaders met us and explained that the minister of education canceled the classes.

It was explained to us that a large religious group had just been there, and their worship and teaching was like nothing the people had ever experienced. There was much screaming and rolling on the floor, which frightened and confused the Russian people, and the Ministry of Education was notified.

The leaders of our team asked to meet with some of the Russian education team and showed and explained the curriculum that the Jesus Film leaders had put together. After about three hours of our team praying while they met, we were notified that our teaching sessions would take place in both cities we were assigned to.

Quite a few of us and our teachers cried and hugged at the farewell time, and I still enjoy looking at the pictures of those meetings. My group of teachers in the second city had the same feelings and emotions as the first, and we had a precious time together.

The Jesus film was shown to each of the teacher groups, and most of them prayed and asked Jesus to be their Savior and Lord, which brought a close bond between us. I cannot explain the awesome joy and satisfaction of teaching the Savior's love and sacrifice for us and for them.

My teacher group in the next city wrote a song for me, and at the farewell celebration, sang it to me using the melody of *My Bonny Lies Over the Ocean*. Here are the words to it, and I cried as the meaning sank in:

Your country lies over the ocean. Your country lies over the sea. Our hearts were closed to the message of God, and we thought you were our enemy.

Our country lies over the ocean. Our country lies over the sea. The darkness was heavy and draining, we could not explain our great need.

Your country lies over the ocean. Your country lies over the sea. You brought us the truth of God's word. We heard it, and now we believe.

I always cry when sharing this, and even now I have tears in my eyes, remembering the feelings on both sides. What an awesome chance to share God's love and forgiveness in a country I never imagined to be in, especially to bring the good news of God.

This is why I love the teaching "Whoever will call upon the name of the Lord will be saved. How then shall they call upon Him in whom they have not believed? And how shall they believe in Him whom they have not heard? And how shall they hear without a preacher? And how shall they preach unless they are sent? Just as it is written: how beautiful are the feet of those who bring glad tidings of good news!"

Once a year I write this scripture to my supporters, reminding them that the only reason I can do what the Lord has called me to is because they make it possible for me to go. God makes them able to give and be on my team and makes me able to go and preach His Word. I thank them with all my heart for sending me.

What an excellent plan, a plan that was made before God made the world. It was made before any of us where in this life and before many of us belonged to Him. Both in Russia and in the Ukraine, I enjoyed the castles and cathedrals, with those beautiful gold-colored gables; they all seemed like you are in one of those many fairy tales.

The story of how the city of Kiev got started is fascinating. One of the stacks of pictures I have is about the three Viking brothers and their sister who discovered the beautiful area where Kiev had its start.

One day, our team was taken to Yalta, which is on the shores of the black sea and has a fascinating history. The wonderful historic castle with its life-size lions I will never forget. I'm grateful for the many pictures to remind me of it all. Both Russia and Ukraine have such a romantic and yet violent history, and it touched my heart when I read their stories.

The India trip

Having been overseas so many times, I want to share only four of the trips. One of those I fell in love with was India. Besides my time mostly in New Delhi, enjoyable was Agra, where we stood in awe of the indescribable Taj Mahal. The following week in Bangalore, I got to interview an amazing pastor who had started several churches using the Jesus film.

Being able to live in most of my trips with Campus Crusade staff made it special because there was an instant feeling of family. There were many chances for us to show our beloved Jesus film, but I want to share only some of the special ones.

It was scheduled for us to show the Jesus film in a village but were warned that there were marauding bands that would come and attack sometimes, stealing things and abusing people. We started out toward that village but had to use tricycles to get there, except for a small old jeep for another lady and me to travel in. The roads were narrow and very rocky.

All of a sudden, it began to rain and then pour with thunder and lightning. We pulled over and had to decide if we should continue since we obviously could not show the film. We felt the Holy Spirit wanted us to notify them that we would try again the next day, so we continued.

As we got close to the village, the rain and thunder stopped, and by the time we parked, the sky was totally clear. We were welcomed by an elderly woman graciously waving us in. They gave us a tour, and we were impressed by how very clean the small huts were, each with a ring of stones for cooking in the center.

At dusk, the people began to gather, and our small film team started setting up. As in most showings, I was surrounded by children, and one of our team translated their questions and my answers.

The team member with perfect knowledge of the dialect gave a short description of the film and opened in prayer. The film showing began, and as always, the viewers were watching the film with great attention, and the children cried at the crucifixion.

At the changing of the reels, I had been asked to give my testimony again with someone translating for me. After the showing, we always ask the people who had said the salvation prayer to come to the lights. We gave them a Gospel of Luke and prayed for them at their request.

We pass out little sheets of paper for them to write down their name and address, but in some countries, many can't write, or they are afraid to put their name down on anything. Most ask for prayer afterward, and it is hard to keep it short because they are serious about this newfound God.

My video of our departure shows the children following us to the edge of the village, and you can see the rain beginning to fall. We had taught them that *hallelujah* means "praise God," and they were following us, shouting "Hallelujah, Hallelujah!" as we started to pull away. Just a minute later, we were driving back into the pouring rain as the sky had totally closed up again.

The blessed trips to Jordan and Israel

Meeting a Jordanian Jesus film staff and his wife visiting at my best friend's church was a great blessing. We met and became friends right away and made plans to see each other again.

My vacation was coming up the following month, and my new friends invited me to spend it with them in Amman, Jordan. We met the following day at the San Clemente pier, and I purchased my tickets for this trip.

It all came together perfectly, and I was excited and started to pack soon. My ministries were already worked out with special people taking my place for those two weeks. Once in Amman, my new friends had arranged a luncheon where I would speak to a group of Christian women in their city.

What an enjoyable time with these sisters in the Lord, and the following day, it was set up for me to speak to women at their church. Two more speaking luncheons were planned for me to share my testimony, and I loved being with these generous and kind Jordanian women.

On one of the days, a special Jesus film showing was set up for a group of Iraqi refugees. These refugees were waiting for their Jordanian citizen ship and worked at odd jobs, mostly in the fields.

My special friend was the head of the Jordanian Jesus Film and arranged that showing. At the changing of the reels, my testimony was to be given with an interpreter, to which I happily agreed. So at noontime, four of us took off planning for the film showing by six o'clock, when these refugees would be back from the fields.

Well, our trip took us more and more downhill, and it got more and more hot. We drove by a very large stone that had a zero painted on it. One of my precious three buddies said, "Hannah, from here on we are with the fish." They explained that from here on, we were below sea level, and we kept going down toward the Jordan Valley. This is the lowest place on earth, 1,371 feet below sea level.

Suddenly my driver said, "Hannah, get your passport ready," and I was shocked. Confused, I told them about not having brought my passport, figuring that we were in Jordan and were showing the film in Jordan. Now, my partners were shocked and explained that the showing would be next to the Israeli border.

They told me that we had to pass four Israeli checkpoints where the guards would make us get out of the car and request our passports, telling me not only that but also they would search through the entire car.

Next, they would even search us; the whole thing usually takes at least thirty minutes. This would get us just in time to the planned Jesus film showing because there are three more checkpoints to cross.

As we got close to the station, I saw that these guards each carried a rifle, and the middle one had it in his hand. The guys were worried because they could not leave me in no-man's-land, and turning back would mean to give up on ministering to these thirty-five refugees. Well, as always, our beloved God knew that His daughter had no passport, so He had planned ahead.

There was no turning around now because we arrived at the guard shack. When the guard bent down to look into the car, the tip of the rifle was right in our driver's face. He looked at every one, a little longer at me, while our driver explained that I was from the United States.

To our great surprise, the guard stepped back and waved his hand for us to move on. My three partners' mouths dropped open. They were totally surprised and said that this has never happened before. These guards were known to have no mercy in not passing a car without total search or even refusing passage. We were praising God with all our hearts.

This was not our last surprise because thanks to our merciful God, the same thing happened at the next three checkpoints. My beloved film team had a hard time believing the miracles, and we sang praise songs to our God.

Well, when we arrived at the area of the film showing, it was in a what they call a small courtyard surrounded by four buildings. The refugees began to arrive straight from the fields, not having had time for dinner yet, and our film is two hours long, plus time for the reel changes.

To our great surprise, after the 35 had arrived, our viewers kept coming and coming until we counted 142 of them. We were totally praising our awesome God, while our guests seated themselves on the dirt floor.

There was no place for me to sit when suddenly two of the men brought me a big, old upholstered chair and set it next to me. Thanking them while sitting down, I realized that there was some strange movement in my seating equipment and tried real hard not to imagine what might be living in there.

I was a little nervous about being asked to open in prayer, but then I was relieved when one of my teammates offered to interpret. It was so awesome to be with these Iraqi men, many of them in turbans. Showing the Jesus film and explaining salvation to them was awesome, and to this day, I enjoy the video of it. Even though the films were on VHS cassettes, I had them made into DVDs.

This was a total blessing when, after the showing, the viewers were asked who prayed the salvation prayer, and almost every hand went up. Some of the men asked my film team something, and they told me that the men wanted me to pray for them.

Agreeing and asking for an interpreter, the prayers flowed. However, it took a whole hour before one of our team member closed in prayer so we could leave for home at midnight.

We were singing praise songs to our beloved God all the way back home. When we asked these men who wanted to learn more about this Jesus, all the hands went up again. Two of our team volunteered to do follow-up with Bible studies in that area, and we all prayed for extra energy and wisdom over these two men.

Someone had confided in us to take a different way home, it was through two villages; it would take longer, but we avoided the checkpoints. We got home at three in the morning, tired but so blessed about God's faithfulness and His total protection once again.

Five days later, I was going to visit a Christian brother and his family in Bethlehem. The first time I visited these Campus Crusade staff, we fell in love with each other, and we drew up mock adoption papers. The two times before, he picked me up at the Tel Aviv airport. This time, however, I was coming from Jordan on a bus.

Going across the Jordanian border was more than I had imagined. It took a very long time to clear everyone's papers at the crossing point. So by this time, it was already late afternoon, and my friend and I were going to meet at noon at the Jerusalem Square.

When the bus left everyone off at the Damascus Gate, I was not able to reach my friend by phone. Instead of worrying this time, I bought myself a falafel sandwich, which is my favorite. Sitting down on a bench and enjoying my sandwich, I asked the Holy Spirit to show me His plan.

About fifteen minutes later, a voice called my name, and here was my Bethlehem friend. He had figured, when he did not hear from me, to just come back to our designated meeting place. These friends were Campus Crusade staff and were nationals. Most of these new believers were rejected by their families because their faith was in Jesus Christ now.

We had five days of blessed ministry and Bible studies, some at other homes, and some at his. It was a never-to-be-forgotten time with these brothers and sisters in Christ and their unbelievable faith and trust in God. At the end of my time there, we said a sad farewell, and I headed back to Jordan.

When the bus let me off at the station, I looked for my Jordanian friend but could not find him. An hour later, I had to find a taxi because the last bus for Amman had already left for the day. The taxi looked like a very old and well-used one, and cramped in on either side of me were two men with four behind me and four more in front.

Taking a deep breath, I claimed my Savior's promise to never leave me or forsake me and got ready for an hour-and-a-half ride to Amman. While praying and remembering some verses, suddenly a sweet voice hit my ears saying, "Mom, what are you doing in here?"

Let me explain something. I have twelve adopted sons. These were Jesus Film leaders in their country, and I supported their precious ministries monthly. Being in their country, I got to stay with them and their families, and we adopted each other so they called me Mom, and their children called me Grandma, and I loved it.

Well, back to my ride on the Jordanian border, the bus had left me out on the wrong side of the station. My friend, being one of those adopted sons, was at the other side anxiously looking for me. My heavenly bridegroom was not going to leave me in that taxi, and so I was found. My precious friend and I were praising and worshipping our God all the way back to Amman.

Botswana/Africa

Another of my memorable trips was to Botswana, Africa. My friends warned my boss about letting me go. They said I would never stop, and they proved to be right. We got to stay at a lovely single-story motel full of those colorful African flowers and plants, and since the temperature was perfect, we got to eat all our meals on the romantic patio.

In the daytime, we would go to the stores and markets, ask to speak with the manager and, with permission, would share the four spiritual laws. We also gave them a Jesus film in their language and prayed the sinner's prayer with them.

Not only was the permission to share Christ given each time, but a moment later, we were surrounded by many more of the staff. To our great surprise, they also wanted to pray the sinner's prayer with us. As we left each of the stores, a few of the employees followed us out and wanted to know more.

Being prayed for was always the greatest desire every-where we witnessed, and they appreciated our material. The supply of Jesus films we had brought were never enough, and we promised to be back the next day with more.

We were utterly blessed and could not believe their hunger for God and began to visit the open market places, which were set up in the middle of town. Here, also many of the costumers followed us, asking us questions as we shared God's story of His love and great gift of salvation.

Our leaders for our group were Jim and Juanita Wyatt, and they arranged a short meeting after breakfast before we left for town. With prayers and some songs, we felt ready for warfare. The song we sang most has since then become my favorite and is "The Days of Elijah."

In the evenings, the three Campus Crusade local staff would have Jesus film showings set up for us. We were blessed and encouraged by the big crowds, coming early and staying after to be prayed for. It was such a joy for me to share my testimony each time at the changing of the film reels with an interpreter. I often enjoy the DVD of these showings.

One of the churches and their pastor were working with us and asked me to come on Sunday and speak at the service. It was awesome to hear about and see their great outreaches to this very large area. Once again, my video shows all the hands raised, testifying of the salvation prayer. Part of my tithing goes to this church, and I receive the reports of their growth.

Just one more trip

At another Jesus film showing in India, we had permission for a showing and were once again welcomed by the elders. They showed us the location of the movie event and told us that the only electric outlet for our projector was in their temple. With the help of the two local film team members, the screen was hung right over one of their gods.

This god was a statue of a very large black cow, which was now covered up by our film screen. Here was the Jesus film running, and behind it and all around the screen were statues of their different gods.

It was like a miracle to us because it was done with full permission of the elders of that village. The showing was a big success as always, and almost everyone in that village received Jesus Christ as Savior and Lord.

Afterwards, we were invited to visit a few of the homes, and most of them had their walls full of pictures of their gods, except the home of the two film team members who were cousins. Before we left, I was asked to pray for their families, and we all held hands and gave God thanks and praise for it all.

The cows came to watch the film with us, and we were not allowed to chase them away because they were holy. What a total joy and blessing to be used of the Lord in these places, also in the airports while waiting for our flight transfers, and on the airplanes. What great remembrance all these pictures and videos are. What glory they give to our God.

Bill and the rainstorm

In 2007, my youngest son, Bill, and his wife, Carol, decided to move with their two children to Kentucky, where her parents followed them. My missing them was indescribable, and so I saved up all my change during the year, and they payed half the fare. This way, I can go visit them once a year when the kids are out of school

One year, it was 2008, after another sad farewell, Bill loaded me up for the airport. Usually, the whole family comes along for one more nice picnic together. However, this time it was unusually cold, and the rain was pouring down, so Bill and I went alone.

Leaving earlier than usual because we had to drive slow, when we got to Lexington, the rain was pouring even heavier. Getting ready to make a left turn into the street that would get us to the airport, Bill slowed down. We were in the most right of the three lanes, which were turning with us. This miracle is so hard to describe, and I hope you can follow my picture.

We started to turn and were almost finishing the left turn when our car kept on sliding left, crossing in front of the cars next to us. The car jumped over the big cement divider in the middle of the street, into the opposite oncoming traffic lanes. It was after-work hours, so all those lanes had full traffic.

Putting my hands over my eyes tightly, calling out the name of Jesus several times, I waited for any of those cars to hit us. After one more sharp jerk to the left, the car stopped very suddenly. Opening my eyes and in shock, as was Bill,

I saw that we had landed in the left turning lane of the opposite side.

In awe, we realized that our amazing God had let us slide across three lanes, with heavy traffic, and over a large cement intersection. We were now in the opposite lane, and He never allowed one of all those cars to even touch us. Bill and I were hugging, praising, and thanking our God. I even got to my departure on time with a memorable flight home.

Losing my mom

In May 1995 my beloved mom was diagnosed with cancer, and when they did a surgery, they found out it was too late. The doctors sent her home to die with her family instead of in the hospital. We took turns reading the scriptures to her, and she was greatly comforted by all of the Lord's promises.

I kept asking my trustworthy Father if He would heal her, but most of all, keep her from pain, and miraculously, she had none. It was comforting to sit with her, read Scriptures, and keep her spirit up. One night, my sister, Karin, had just put her to bed when she realized that she was not breathing. Karin and her husband, Harold, rushed to her room and realized that our mom had quietly slipped into the arms of Jesus.

We all miss her very much, but knowing we would be together with her and Jesus someday soothed our pain. Her absence left a big hole in our lives, and we meet together as often as possible.

Losing my sister

It was almost the same story with my younger sister, Karin. She also was diagnosed with cancer, being told that there was nothing else they can do for her and sent her home with pain pills and chemo. Again, I had the chance to sit with her for hours every day, hold her hand, and read and explain the Word of God to her in the Holy Spirit's presence.

She went to be with her Lord on January 2011. Like my mom, she also left us in her sleep, and we know for sure that she, like our mom, is waiting for the rest of us to join her.

There were also grandparents, my former husband, one granddaughter, six great-grandchildren, my dad, seven uncles, six aunts, and one son-in-law who were expecting us. What a great homecoming celebration this will be, and all this because of the great love of our awesome God who patiently waited for us.

Another fall and healing

On my way home from a meeting, I made a strong turn, trying to get up some stairs, when the front of my right shoe got caught under the heal of the left one, and I went down hard. Landing with my left shoulder on the bottom step of the staircase, the pain was great. Having trouble raising myself up, someone had already dialed 911, and the ambulance was there in no time.

The available physician had immediate x-rays ordered and came in with them to show and explain the outcome.

He said that the hip is just badly bruised, but the left shoulder is broken and needs surgery as soon as possible. He prescribed strong pain pills and an arm sling because it was too painful to lift my arm even a little.

The following Monday, I watched *The 700 Club*, and at the end of the program, Terry and Pat were praying for people. Suddenly Terry said, "There is a lady who had a fall and badly injured her left shoulder, not being able to lift her arm at all. The Lord is healing that shoulder right now, so begin lifting your arm and keep trying until the hand reaches the back of the head."

Laughing out loud, I told the Lord that I claim that healing and began to lift my arm little by little, higher and higher. Within half an hour, I was swinging that arm around and around like a pitcher does his baseball. Performing that evening before some of my family, they persuaded me to cancel my surgery, which was scheduled in three days.

I have the x-rays and the report of this wonderful healing, and I was praising my beloved God with every move made. My doctor was amazed and canceled the procedure and made an appointment to make some x-rays so he could close the case. There have been no problems or any pain since then, and I am still praising my Lord and Savior now, five years later.

Kayla's fishing miracle

The count was nineteen great-grandchildren now, and my precious supporters made it possible for me to buy a van. This way, I could take seven of them to church on Wednesdays because their parents worked.

They could also come with me on different trips or to church programs like AWANA, a wonderful youth program at Immanuel Baptist and many churches. God allowed me to work with middle-school age on Sunday nights and high-school age on Monday nights.

All my grands and great-grands liked fishing, and on this particular trip, my daughter, Lita, brought her own car because she and two of the girls had to leave earlier than Kayla and I had planned to. Lita and her girls asked if we could go to a different part of lake Gregory this time, and I saw no reason not to.

However, it turned out to be quite crowded, so we had to be closer to a wall the lake was enclosed by on that side.

The girls were very intrigued by that high wall, and looking down the wall, we saw that it went straight down into the water and that it was packed with seaweed. I explained to the young ladies that this would be a dangerous place to fall in because they would not be able to swim out for the seaweed would tangle around their feet and arms.

When Lita and her girls packed their stuff to leave, the girls moved my chair closer to the dirt area where Kayla was fishing. A short lady was sitting down about six feet to my right on a park bench. Kayla had given her one of our little yellow witnessing booklets called *The Four Spiritual Laws*, as was our habit to do.

While reaching into the car, which was parked next to mine, to get more paper, Kayla had come up to the wall area. As I got my arms out of the front seat, Kayla was swinging her fishing pole round and round, and with a yip, disappeared down the wall.

Never having moved this fast before, I realized with a sick feeling that, even though I was an excellent swimmer, there would be no way to swim through the seaweed. Getting to the edge of the wall, I saw that Kayla was not in the water but stood on a two-feet round pile of gravel that the waves must have pushed against the wall.

Realizing that even if I lay flat on the floor, and being five feet seven inches, having long arms, there would be no way to reach her hand to pull her up. Everyone else had left; there was no one I could ask for help.

Suddenly the little lady from the park bench lay next to me and reached for Kayla's hand; her arm seemed to stretch longer and longer, and with a quick jerk, she had my precious girl up and in my arms.

When we both turned our heads to thank her, there was no one in the entire about-fifty-feet surrounding area. We looked down and saw that the pole had floated away and that the two-feet gravel pile was no longer there either.

Kayla and I kept hugging and thanking our beloved Savior with all our heart, realizing that the lady had to have been an angel.

My next fall and healing

My youngest son, Bill, and his family had been with us from Kentucky for a visit, and I had just dropped them at the airport for their flight home. Kayla and I were hungry, so before heading back home, we found a place to eat. We were close to the door when, suddenly, I slipped and went down hard, hitting my tailbone, hip, and head.

Being in pain and because I could not move, someone called 911. Their arrival was four minutes. I was grateful for that. The medics were very kind to Kayla, who was crying. She had never seen me hurt.

When the MRI was done, the doctor said that there could not be a hip surgery because the metal piece from the previous hip replacement left no room for another screw.

He continued saying that they could not do surgery on my lower spine either because it was too shattered and deteriorated. It would take lying still in bed for six to eight weeks for the break to heal. Showing the report to my regular physician and two friends who were nurses, all they could say was, "Oh, Hannah."

They gave me the DVD and the written report of it all to show my pastor, friends, and children. There was a very special time of learning that came to me during those six weeks I had to lie in bed.

The opportunity to hear the teachings of some Christian pastors in the mornings on TBN was an unbelievable blessing, by learning things presented that I had never heard in this way before.

Making sure of the truth by using my Bible along with them, the joy and blessings just flowed. My relationship with my beloved God and Savior became closer than I ever thought possible, receiving a freedom from guilt that was greater than it had ever been.

Of course, I zealously made sure that everything they taught came from the Word of God. Asking for prayer from the church elders, as the Bible tells us to, my hip and tail bone were healed. The following x-rays showed no damage at all, and once again, I have the x-ray and the report. Praise to my God for letting me be full-time back in ministry after eight weeks.

Carol's back surgery and healing

Shortly before my yearly October visit with Bill and Carol and their kids in Kentucky, I got a call from Carol. She was crying and asked for prayer and said she had been to her doctor this day.

He performed a lengthy examination and finally told her that she needed to see a lung specialist. Having had cancer before, her mind was alarmed. We prayed together, and I reminded her that this was not a surprise to the God who loved her very much.

Lifting her up before our Savior was a privilege for me because she had become a young sister to me since Bill first brought her home. We all prayed together while we waited for the next verdict from the specialist. My request for three weeks' vacation instead of the original one week was okayed, making me glad I could be there for them.

The verdict came after two more tests, and it was worse than we could have imagined. The specialist explained that she had a tumor the size of a grapefruit in the lobe of her left lung. There is a great risk in doing the scheduled surgery because the lobe was putting pressure against the heart.

The surgery lasted seven hours, as they removed this very large tumor and half of her lung. The tumor showed up to be cancerous, but no chemo or radiation was needed because the tumor was "encapsulated." We rejoiced because God answered our prayers for a safe operation, and we thanked Him with all our hearts. This all took place on her birthday, and we celebrated after she got home.

The doctor tried to prepare us that sometimes these tumors come back, but I knew that this one would not. It has been nine years now, and there has not been the slightest sign of a growth of any kind. The three weeks there with Bill's family was a real blessing, especially Carol, as she learned much more of the love and faithfulness of her God.

The football players at Moby Gym

It was time again for the every-other-year staff training in Fort Collins at the Colorado State University. It was the best place to house the over five thousand Campus Crusade for Christ US staff. The rest of our staff have been ministering in other countries all over the world.

This biannual staff training is something I look forward to for two years, and each time, it seems to be better than the time before. As usual the morning worship and speakers were a true joy and a chance for spiritual growth.

The dorm rooms are comfortable, and the roommate is always a staff sister, and the meals are served in a very nice cafeteria close by. It was dinnertime, and I was waiting for my coworkers to join me. The table next to mine began to be filled with big football players who lived at this university.

They started out being six of them and, little by little, added three more at the table on the other side of mine. Suddenly the Holy Spirit influenced me that the young men could really use our Jesus film.

Going over to the football players' tables, I introduced myself, stating who all these peoples in the room were. Mentioning the name of our organization, I explained that we also represent a movie made in 1,200 languages by now.

Showing them the one I had, I said that it was made in the Holy Land and by the Gospel of Luke. I continued that each DVD had the two-hour film in twenty-four languages, asking if they would each like a DVD.

In the meantime, three more joined the group, making it twelve altogether. Asking them where I could meet them to hand over the movies the following day, they said the best time and place would at eleven o'clock on the ground floor of Moby Gym.

Realizing I had only one DVD left, I began to call some of my Jesus film coworkers, and together we came up with twelve movies. The next morning, I took a seat at the ground floor of the gym and, at eleven o'clock, went to the area I was told their gym was located.

To my disappointment, no one was there, so I waited half an hour; and when the janitor arrived, he said he was not informed of them being here this day.

Returning to my seat in Moby, I asked the Lord to let me somehow find at least one of these players to give my bag of movies to. Trying hard to focus and listen to the current speaker, I suddenly had the strong impression to take my bag of DVDs and go outside the door.

Following that sense, I went and opened the door, and just then, all twelve players passed by. Laughing, they stopped, apologized for the time change, and surrounded me, each gratefully accepting his Jesus film.

Over the years, I have learned to pay close attention to these impressions and promptings, having learned from Scripture and a few experiences that this is one of the ways the Lord speaks to us.

Shiloh congregation

Five years ago, picking up my car from the scheduled oil change, I noticed a lady also waiting to pick up hers. Starting a conversation, the subject came to our beliefs. Mentioning being a missionary with Campus Crusade for Christ brought a big smile because she knew of the organization.

We introduced ourselves, and she told me she attended a Messianic congregation named Shiloh. She invited me to visit, and I promised to do that. At my first visit, I was blessed by the one and a half hours of awesome worship of Yeshua—we say Jesus—and then some powerful teaching from the Word of God.

After attending for a year, on the third Saturday of the month, I have had the privilege of co-teaching about fifteen children. The eight-to-twelve-year-old ones are attentive and full of questions. What a joy, and it has been five years now. I look forward to attending there Saturdays and Immanuel on Sundays, and that is not all.

The Way World Outreach

Six years ago, my son, Steve, and his wife started to attend her church called the Way World Outreach. I loved it and got totally involved. My daughters joined them, then two of my grandsons with their spouses and all their children.

On Wednesday evening, seven of my great-grandchildren had no way to church that night. Well, the Lord had just given me a big Toyota van where I could take the seven to Wednesday night service.

There were nine adults attending now, only five on Wednesdays, and the young people were in their own classes, really liking it. So when the Lord told me to take my great-grandchildren on Wednesdays, I was obedient and got blessed. Hallelujah!

My stroke

Coming out of the elevator from my doctor's appointment, I suddenly realized that the left side of my body was weak. Embarrassed because of my walk, it looked like I was drunk, I continued to my car and drove home. Feeling very weak and going to bed right away, sleep came quickly.

However, the next morning, I realized that something was very wrong. Not being able to rise, I called my friend, Charlene, who took me to the closest emergency center. My speech was slurry, but she understood me, and when we entered the clinic and she mentioned what was wrong, the doctor responded immediately.

The ambulance of that clinic had just returned, and they were able to take me to my hospital, where I was instantly placed in a room. There was no pain, so the whole thing did not seem very real, but I wondered what was going on.

After a CAT scan, they saw a blood clot in the Basal Ganglia above my ear on the right side of my head and informed me of that. After a second CAT scan and two more tests, I was registered in the hospital and was put in a more permanent room.

Sadly, it was a single room, and no chance for a room-mate; however, after the third day, they transferred me by ambulance to a nearby rehabilitation center. There was still absolutely no pain, so it all still did not seem real to me, especially since my speech was back to normal now.

The rehab time was to be one month, and I was informed by the doctor on duty what to expect. Everything was very clean, and I got to meet a great team of nurses and aides who were kind and helpful. There were many times I could share about the God I loved and also was able to pass out some Christian literatures and many of the Jesus films.

After one week at the rehab center, I had already been doing everything on my own, including walking daily once around the inside of the building and more. I enjoyed the physical therapy and bought a small stationary bike to use at home.

When I reported all this to the doctor and mentioned that one of my daughters and one of my sons lived with me at this time, I was released. The doctor informed me that a therapist and a nurse would visit me for three more weeks till all was satisfactory.

With my GMO ministry, which is answering e-mails from all over the world, I was able to continue the day after coming home. After another week, my juvenile hall ministry could be continued; and four days later, I was back in my middle school ministry.

The pregnancy center ministry I was not able to continue until two weeks after my release because it requires the most walking. The things needed for each client have to be picked up for her in the storage room. I could also now continue to take my great-grandchildren to Wednesday night service at their church again.

Everyone, including my doctors, were amazed. They, being believers, agreed with me that it was the Lord's doing, and all who knew me once again rejoiced with me.

The middle school ministry

In 2014 my church adopted one of the local middle schools, planning to help with some equipment and a young man to assist with sports. The church also hoped to have someone to give Bible studies. The youth pastor knew of my ministry to different youth groups and in juvenile hall for twenty-seven years.

He let me know the need, and after my agreeing, he signed me up. The first time at the school, the principal asked me if it would be all right for me to come and teach every day. Needing to decline because of my job with the Jesus film and the pregnancy center on Wednesdays, I promised to be there for two hours every Tuesday and Thursday.

This teaching is for students who stay after school for a program called CAPS. These students stay because their parents work, and this program has several classes for them to choose from. One is sports or cooking or music or crafting and my class, which the school calls Alive class. A picture of our class will be in the yearbook again.

Usually, anywhere from eight to fifteen students come, and I enjoy teaching the Word of God. In the past four years, I also had one to four of my great-grandchildren attend at this school and will have some more coming. What a tremendous joy and blessing this is to me, knowing it is a gift from God.

After my children were grown and gone from home, I asked my beloved God to minimize my motherly feelings, figuring these feelings were much less needed now, so He could shrink them, but instead He keeps giving me more and more children.

God's protection again

There have been so many times of the Lord taking care of us; I could not possibly tell them all, but here is one more. It was after Christmas, and it was now time to remove the decorations from the top of the TV cabinet. Taking some in my hand and stepping back, the heal of my shoe got caught on the rug behind me.

Falling backwards, my upper body was headed for the coffee table straight in back of me. Calling out my Savior's name several times, my body suddenly turned. Instead of my head and shoulders hitting the coffee table, they now landed on the cushions of the couch to my right.

My son and two of my great-granddaughters saw the whole event and, just as myself, sat silent for a minute. I was totally amazed as were they, having seen my whole body make a fifteen-degree turn in the last moment and not hit the table. The table was heavy wood with a large glass center. Very gratefully I thanked my God, and when I realized that there was no pain, my son helped me to get up.

There was no way to explain this because it happened so fast. I could not have consciously made my body turn. There had to be a loving hand turning my body to the right and toward the couch.

From the beginning of my life with the Lord, I have loved the verse "Delight yourself in the Lord, and He will give you the desire of your heart." However, knowing myself, I did not trust the desires of my heart, so I always pray, "Give me the desire of Your heart." This turned out to be a very safe prayer because He proved Himself to be worthy.

Another angel?

A friend gave a testimony at devotion time of a close relation of hers. This lady was driving home from work on a rainy and very foggy night. Suddenly she saw someone waving her down, and she hit the brakes, swerving some on the wet road. She grabbed her flashlight and got out but saw no one at all.

Pointing the flashlight straight ahead, she noticed something in the road. Going closer, she recognized a car on her side of that highway she was on. She could see now that the car was upside down and that there were people in it.

Thanking God for her iPhone, she dialed 911, and coming even closer, realized that the four people in the car were knocked out cold. Help arrived soon, and she stood next to her car, realizing in tears that she would have smashed directly into that turned-over car.

She thanked the Lord with all of her heart for that, for what she believed was an angel, waving her down. Every one hearing her testimony had tears in their eyes as they agreed with her about God's amazing protection.

San Bernardino Pregnancy Resource Center

In 2009, I heard of the pregnancy center having lost five of their advocates. These are women who volunteer, pray with, and supply pregnant women with the needs for their babies. It is a very important and meaningful ministry provided for expecting mothers or women with young children up to the age of two.

Most of these mothers are single and are very short on income, so they cannot supply their children with many of the things needed. There are about between 300 to 350 women a month that come for help, and it is a joy to be able to provide for them. It is also very meaningful to pray with them, for which they are very grateful, often with tears.

One time, I had a client and her boyfriend, who were living in his car because he had lost his job, and she was pregnant. She was crying the whole time, so I had to speak with him. We kept them in the center until we found a place for her and a place for him.

Since they were not married yet, they could not live in the same shelter together. but we encouraged them to get married when they can at the Hall of Records, which has a lovely chapel, and once the papers are filled out, the judge will do the ceremony at the cost of ninety-eight dollars. I told them to help with the money if they really wanted to spend their life together.

One young couple came for a pregnancy test and were delighted at the test being positive. At the second appointment, I found out what their needs were so we could help them. Telling them how much God loves them and their baby and explaining the awesome salvation plan of God, they wanted Jesus as their Savior and Lord.

We were about to close our time in prayer when they discussed something and suddenly asked me if I would please teach them the Bible. After agreeing happily, we made out a time and day for these studies. It was such a joy to teach them because of their total amazement about His great love and forgiveness.

When their little son was born, they asked me to be the baby's godmother, and I got to meet her loving family. His parents live in Mexico and were not able to be there at this time. When we are willing, we will never know of the ways our Lord will use us and have some joyful surprises coming.

We have been able to help thousands at the pregnancy center, and our clients did not have to abort their babies because we were able to fill some of their needs. It is hard for us to express the feeling of satisfaction when our time at the center is done for the day. We are grateful because God makes it all possible.

Well, I am only eighty now, and the Lord willing will never retire but that my ministries keep increasing. My twenty great-grandchildren are a joy to me. They are the ages between twenty-one years down to one year.

All of them are around me except for Jaxson, my twentieth great-grandchild, who lives with his parents in Kentucky. This is where my youngest son moved his family to, and I go visit there once a year. They all know Jesus from the Bible studies with me, except little Jaxson who will be taught by his parents and grandparents. They all attend a good Bible teaching church and spend time daily in the Word of God.

One more ministry

One of the minor ministries my great-grandchildren and I have had for so many years is what we call our Park Ministry. This has been where we go to different parks, have fun, and pass out the booklets called *The Four Spiritual Laws* or the *Beginning Your Journey of Joy*, which were both written by Dr. Bill Bright.

Hardly anyone has turned them down, but sometimes people will come up and talk to me about the booklets and their content. Their distribution of tens of thousands in juvenile hall has been a real joy. The turnaround for these young prisoners is anywhere from two to six months, so they get at least eight Bible studies a month before leaving.

Campus Crusade has produced the four laws without staples in them because my young prisoners are not allowed to have staples. The *Beginning Your Journey of Joy* booklets are mauve and pettier for girls, but the staples need to be removed. Both kinds have the same content and are really treasured by the young people, as they are the only thing they can have in their cell.

The Four Spiritual Laws booklet is what I was saved with, having passed them out since then because they contain the prayer of salvation. Even at the airports and on the planes, people receive them or allow me to read them; hardly anyone turns them down.

Oh, what a blessing, and it is not finished until the Lord says it is time to come home, for which I wait with all my heart. Wishing still to be more perfect in the spiritual, I continue to spend daily time in my Beloved's Word, never stopping to learn and grow. My favorite verse says that I am my Beloved's, and He is mine, and this has gotten me through everything.

The teaching most important to me is encouraging everyone to read the Word of God every day. I use this subject also in the Global Media Outreach (GMO) ministry, where people from all over the world tell us that they have received Jesus as their Savior and Lord.

Now, we get to tell them what is the next step, and for me, number one is to read God's Word, the Bible, every day. This is when He began to truly change my life, and I saw this happen to all who listens to God. It is most important to Him because knowing Him is how His beloved children are able to trust Him and love Him.

The Lord promises in Joshua 1:8 and in Psalm 1:1–3 that if you read His Word daily, then you will prosper, and then you will have good success. The thousands of testimonies I have heard of what He will do if you read it every day came from adults and young peoples. I found in my life that knowing God is not enough; falling in love with Him is what brings the growth.

This is what I pray for all I come in touch with, even for those yet to come. Steve's son and his wife will have children, and there is his daughter who is eighteen now. Bill's daughter is getting married in October in Kentucky, and there is his son who is fifteen, so these great-grandbabies do not end for me until the Lord comes. What a joy.

My precious supporters make it possible for me to follow the Lord's call. and I am very grateful to them for listening to Him. It will be my great joy to introduce them to all the brothers and sisters who are in heaven because they sent me to go.

One of my favorite teachers says, "What I focus on grows in me, and what grows in me I become." I love this and think on this daily because it has proven to be true. The more I read His Word, the more my Savior is on my mind, and the closer my relationship with Him develops.

I pray with all my heart that this account has been of help, showing how very faithful our God is in raising our children, grands, and great-grands. We must give them to Him and then trust Him with them. Sometimes I take them back and worry, but that happens less and less as I see His faithfulness.

He is involved in everything that concerns us, as you have heard in the great variety in my life. You can never imagine how God will use you if you give your life to Him. It will be your greatest blessing and joy.

Just because I'm eighty now, there is no slowing down unless my beloved God makes me. I've asked Him to keep me busy if I have to stay here on earth, so we still have some work to do in His harvest. Be ready. The Bible says the fields are white for harvest, and He is looking for workers.

So here I am, Lord. Keep sending me!

About the Author

Having found out who guides and leads her life, Hannah has great joy in helping others to find the only answer to come out of darkness into His marvelous light. Thousands of the youths she taught know now why they are in this world and that God's plan for them is for good, not for evil. Like Hannah, they have read the end of the book.

Having learned and believing that her Savior has defeated the enemy of mankind, and God has therefore transferred her from the kingdom of darkness into the kingdom of His beloved Son, she is now His beloved also. This is what helps her mostly overcome things the enemy throws her way, by using the powerful name of Jesus.

CPSIA information can be obtained
at www.ICGtesting.com
Printed in the USA
FSHW010016250221
78907FS

9 781644 165881